# THE MIRACLES OF *J*ESUS *C*HRIST
## THROUGH BISHOP SAM AHULU

# THE MIRACLES OF JESUS CHRIST

## THROUGH BISHOP SAM AHULU

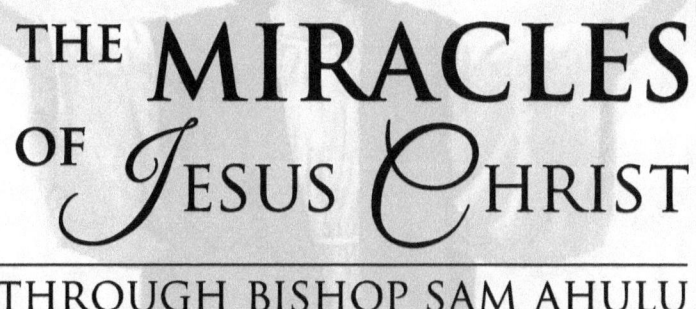

BISHOP SAMUEL AHULU

STONEWALL PRESS
PAVING YOUR WAY TO SUCCESS

*The Miracles of Jesus Christ Through Bishop Sam Ahulu*
Copyright © 2018 by Bishop Samuel Ahulu. All rights reserved.

No part of this publication may be reproduced, stored in a retrieval system or transmitted in any way by any means, electronic, mechanical, photocopy, recording or otherwise without the prior permission of the author except as provided by USA copyright law.

The opinions expressed by the author are not necessarily those of Stonewall Press.

Published in the United States of America

ISBN: 978-1-949362-74-9 (*sc*)
978-1-949362-73-2 (*e*)

Library of Congress Control Number: 2018955105

Published by Stonewall Press
4800 Hampden Lane, Suite 200, Bethesda, MD 20814 USA
1.888.334.0980 | www.stonewallpress.com
1. Religion
2. Spirituality and New Age
18.09.20

# ACKNOWLEDGEMENTS

Okpoti sowah

Late archbishop James M. Temples, Esther Acharige, Shener Stevens

Our Lord and savior, Jesus Christ, the author of it all. Thank God he saw me as an earthly vessel, holy and acceptable in the sight of our Lord and savior Jesus Christ, to be used by him to write this book.

My loving wife, Dorthula, is always there to support and encourage me in prayer, and also alongside me and the members of "the Lord's bible studies."

Thank you all for the prayers and support you have given to me.

God bless you all.

Bishop Samuel Ahulu

## November 8, 2014

### THE FIRST MIRACLE IN AUGUSTA, GEORGIA

This is the first miracle which happened to me in Augusta, Georgia.

I went to attend a family member's wedding when the Holy Spirit started telling me to start writing. I had no pen or paper. I had to call my wife to bring these things. At that time nothing was available, so I started to write on the wedding program.

THE SAMARITAN WOMAN: St. John 4:5-34.

Then cometh he to a city of Samaria, which is called SACHAR, NEAR TO THE PARCEL OF ground that Jacob gave to his son joseph. Jacob's well was there. Jesus, therefore, being wearied with his journey, sat thus on the well and it was about the sixth hour. There cometh a woman of Samaria to draw water. Jesus sayeth unto her, "Give me a drink."

Isaiah 53:4-5: Surely he hath borne our grieves and carried our sorrow, yet we did esteem him stricken, smitten of God and afflicted. But he was wounded for our transgressions. He was bruised for our inequities; the chastisement of our peace was upon him, and with his stripes we are healed.

Zechariah 4:6: then he answered and spoke unto me, saying this is the word of the Lord unto zerubbabel saying, not by might, not by power, but by my spirit, sayeth the Lord of host.

St. John 4:24: the woman of Jacob's well, give me a drink, a simple request, personal evangelism. Not in this mountain thou shall worship the Lord, neither in Jerusalem. Let me tell you salvation is of the Jews. If you knew the one asking you to give him the water, you may ask him to give you living water. The woman asked, "Can I have this water. The Lord asked her to call her husband, and she said, "I have no husband," and Jesus said to her, "thou said the truth; you have no husband, and even the one you are with now is not your husband." And the woman said to him, "Are you greater than our father Jacob, who dug this well; and you being a Jew on earth asking me to give you water? Because the Samaritans have no common dealings with the Jews.

God is a spirit and they that worship him must worship him in spirit and in truth. She ran to the village and told them, "come and see someone who was able to tell me everything. The woman said that the messiah would be coming back and when he comes back he would restore everything." Jesus said, "I am the one speaking to you. I am the one."

It is a blessing. Jesus will return to heaven. St. John 16:25-30 Isaiah 53:1-5

Revelation 22:10

Matthew 7:21-28

The Lord rains on the just and the unjust, but at the end the Lord will separate the sheep and the goat.

Mark 1:15: Jesus's ministry of repentance to you.

Revelation 3:20: behold, I stand at the door and knock. If any man hears my voice, and openeth the door, I will come in to him, and will sup with him and he with me.

The divine head of any church is Jesus Christ. Joshua 2:1-8 Joshua 24:15

And if it seems evil unto you to serve the Lord, choose you this day whom ye will serve, whether the gods which your fathers served that were on the other side of the flood, or the gods of the Amorites in whose land ye dwell, but as for me and my house, we will serve the Lord.

God bless.

Genesis 12:20: the call of Abram. We are all the seed of Abram. Therefore, we are already blessed.

Isaiah 53:1-5: he chooses you, not of yourself. Predestinate: set aside for the Lord. The greatest honor for born again Christians is to. Serve God. I came for those who are in need of a doctor.

St. John 10:10: I am the way, the truth and the life.

St. John 15:13: greater love hath no man than this that a man lay down his life for his friends.

Matthew 11:28: come unto me, all ye that labor and are heavy laden, and I will give you rest.

Isaiah 59:1-2: behold the Lord's hand is not shortened that it cannot save, neither his ear heavy that it cannot hear; but your iniquities have separated between you and your God, and your sins have hid his face from you, that he will not hear.

Isaiah 1:18-19: come now, and let us reason together, sayeth the Lord. Though your sins be as scarlet, they shall be white as snow; though they be red like crimson, they shall be as wool.

St. John 11:25: I am the resurrection and the life, he that believeth in me, though he was dead, yet shall he live.

Exodus 20:1-17: the law was given to Moses, and grace and mercy was given to Jesus Christ, meaning he paid our sins on the cross. We have to surrender all to him, total submission, not partial. Any church without the Holy Spirit means that I am not there. It happened when john the Baptist baptized Jesus in the river Jordan and said, "This is my beloved son in whom I am well pleased."

Matthew 4:14: then he went to the wilderness to be tempted by the devil for 40 days. He said, "If you are truly the son of God, turn these stones into bread," but he answered and said, "It is written, man shall not live by bread alone, but by every w that proceedeth out of the mouth of God." Then again he sent him to the mountain top to be tempted again. He said if I am truly the son of God bow down to me. If you only bow down to me and worship me, I will give you the whole world. Then Jesus said unto him, "get thee hence, Satan; it is written, thou shalt worship the Lord thy God, and him only shalt thou serve."

Mark 1:15: Jesus started his ministry with repentance.

After john accused pharaoh of marrying his brother's wife, they planned to kill him (that is the daughter and the wife) and they brought his head on a plate to the palace. This is when Jesus started his ministry in galilee.

The kingdom of God is at hand. Repent ye therefore, and be baptized every one of you. In my father's house there are a lot of mansions and I go to prepare a place for you, and when I am finished I will come unto you, that wherever I am there you may be also; and if I go, I will send the comforter, which is the holy spirit.

John 14:1-4: let not your heart be troubled; ye believe in God, believe also in me. In my father's house are many mansions, if it were not so, I would have told you. I go to prepare a place for you and if I go and prepare a place for you, I will come again and receive you unto myself, that where I am, there ye may be also. And whither I go, ye know, and the way ye know.

St. John 14:6: Thomas asked, "Are you leaving us, and we don't know the way?" Jesus said "I am the way, the truth and the life; no man cometh unto the father but by me.

God bless. Amen.

Genesis 3:1: now the serpent was more subtle than any beast of the field, which the Lord God had made. And he said unto the woman, "yea, hath God said, ye shall not eat of every tree of the garden?" And the woman said unto the serpent, "we may eat of the fruit of the trees of the garden." Freely eat, but of the fruit of the tree of life thou shall not touch. We inherit sin from our first parents, Adam and eve. One man brought sin into the world and we all became sinners, the first Adam. The second Adam. Jesus Christ took it upon himself to carry our sins to the cross; therefore we all need to come to repentance and to accept him, Jesus Christ, as our personal savior and Lord of our lives. Jesus Christ is calling us all to come to repentance.

Mark 1:15: and saying, the time is fulfilled, and the kingdom of God is at hand. Repent ye and believe the gospel.

Continuation of john the Baptist's ministry. This is the Lamb of God, who came to take the sins of the world upon his shoulders. On the cross he said, "It is finished." We all need to cross the bridge and the cross is the bridge.

Matthew 26:36-46: and he came to the disciples, and said to them, "couldn't you help me for one hour in the garden of gethsemane to watch and pray?" They were all sleeping when Jesus needed help for you and me.

St. John 3:16: for God so loved the world that he gave his only begotten son that whosoever believeth in him should not perish, but have everlasting life.

Jesus was sentenced to death. Luke 23:1-56 St. John 18:1-40

God bless.

*December 20, 2014*

## NEW ROCHELLE

My presence is here, but they do not recognize me, Jesus.

My recognition should be known by everyone. Glory hallelujah.

They do not glorify me when I was in the world. I should be first before anything else. They should call upon me first to bless the whole occasion. I came to die for mankind, but only a few people recognize what I came to do. I will come back to give rewards to those who worship me in spirit and in truth. St. John 4:24. Before anything, I should be recognized as the savior of the world. I carry everyone's burden on my shoulders. I shed my blood to give eternal life to all who believe in me and the one who sent me into the world (my father and your father). I said I will come back again, and my reward will be given to those who endureth to the end. Revelation 22:12-13.

St. John 15:1: I am the true vine, and my father is the husbandman. St. John 15:1-10.

I am calling sinners to repentance. Mark 1:15: and saying, the time is fulfilled, and the kingdom of God is at hand. Repent ye and believe the gospel.

Animal sacrifice is no more, but my blood was shed for all mankind, even for those who rejected me. I will also reject them in front of my father in the kingdom.

Matthew 11:28-30: come unto me, all ye that labor and are heavy laden, and I will give you rest. Take my yoke upon you, and learn of me, for I am meek and lowly in heart, and ye shall find rest unto your souls. For my yoke is easy, and my burden is light.

St. Matthew 16:26-28: for what is a man profited if he shall gain the whole world and lose his own soul? Or what shall a man give in exchange for his works, for the son of man shall come in the glory of his father with his angels. And then he shall reward every man according to his works. Verily I say unto you, there be some standing here, which shall not taste of death, till they see the son of man coming in his kingdom.

My father hath given me power both in heaven and in earth, the key to heaven and hell.

Matthew 28:18-20: and Jesus came and spake unto them, saying, "All power is given unto me in heaven and in earth."

## Wednesday—January 7, 2015

**THE FIG**

Most Christians talk about the fig tree when cursed to die to the ground, yes, and I did it to show an example for Christians who accept me as their personal savior, but do not make an effort to win souls for me. The purpose of my coming into this world, what does it profit a man to gain the whole world and lose his own soul? A man came from heaven and knows my father and your father don't play. All the angels have work to do in the kingdom of God. I came that you must have life. St. John 10:10. Some Christians have taken me for granted, but when they die before they would realize that truly I am alpha and omega, the first and the last.

What did he say about the fig tree? Not the tree, but just an example to the Christians who do not do anything for me, other than to envy those who I have called to do my work. The only thing they know to do is to sit down and criticize my chosen ones.

If you open your heart I will come in, but rather they choose to love the satanic world. Rev. 3:20-21

Acts 2:38-40: I chose Paul because he is a blessing to the gospel. Blessings are coming from me (Jesus) to Sam. Continue to do a good job and more blessings coming to you, Sam.

I gave Sam the name for "the Lord's bible studies." Why do you always have trouble in remembering the name? Because I give it to you in the bathroom. Sam, you are a good person. Your wife should study you and she will know that I have chosen you to be my servant. I give Dorthula to you to work with you. Stephanie is very happy with me (Jesus). She is doing a great job in the kingdom. Stop worrying about her. She doesn't want to come back to this wicked world. I created her very beautiful. Many people don't like her because of her beauty.

Bye, bye, Jesus.

# Tuesday—January 13, 2015

## FIRST MESSAGE FROM THE LORD. TODAY'S BIBLE VERSES.

Matthew 6:33: but seek ye first the kingdom of God, and his righteousness, and all these things shall be added unto you.

St. John 6:63: it is the spirit that quickeneth, the flesh profiteth. Note the words that I speak unto you; they are spirit and they are life.

Acts 2:38: then peter said unto them; repent and be baptized every one of you in the name of Jesus Christ for the remission of sins, and ye shall receive the gift of the Holy Ghost.

St. John 4:6-7: now Jacob's well was there. Jesus, therefore, being wearied with his journey, sat thus on the well and it was about the sixth hour. There cometh a woman of Samaria to draw water; Jesus sayeth unto her, "give me to drink."

Sam, more blessings are coming. I called you to do my work I left behind. Be strong. Never have the fear not to speak the truth. People might despise you and hate you, but I am always there with you and Dorthula. Some of the family members do not like you, Sam, because I gave you a car. That is my reward to you. Do the work I called you to do, and do not let anyone help you. I called you and you alone to do it. I do not share my blessings with just anyone. "Be prepared to travel all over the world to preach me. The invitations will be coming in very soon".

Be patient with Dorthula. She does not understand you in many ways, but one day she will see the truth, Sammy.

Rev. Richard is so afraid of you. That is why he did not want you to preach that Sunday when you were there. He sees the difference between you and him when you preach. Now he hardly ever keeps in touch with you. He is jealous of your gift. He really needs to pray more.

I am the one speaking through Dorthula, not to trust anyone around her.

Sam, be aware and watch your steps. Don't you see, everywhere you go people love you. It is because my light is upon you, and I am always there with you wherever you go.

Peace be here at all times. I am going and will be back again. Bye, bye, Sam.

*Jesus of Nazareth.*

# Friday—January 15, 2015

## MY MORNING PRAYER AT 5:00-6:00 A.M.

I am the Lord God. I am with you (Sam). Follow me everyday in your prayers. I (Jesus) love Dorthula so much. She makes a sacrifice for me, Sam, which no one else could do for my chosen one.

Sam is very different among all other preachers. People would fear him because of my anointing upon him. Whatever I, Sam, say, listen to him. He is not out of his mind. That time has already been gone. He is now a new creature and now living a holy life. I have always been calling people, but they do not want to do the work for me. They only say they love me with their lips, but inside there are no love, as they are saying. I will come back to the world. I will be coming back with my angels from heaven. I saw you when you were strolling about with your sickness. I (Jesus) allow the devil, Lucifer, and the condemned angels to attack you so you will know that you have made a lot of mistakes in your life when I first called you to do my work. Now I have corrected you. Never make the same mistakes again. You should have died through that asthma attack, but I saved your life, because you have the greatest love for me. Continue the good work I have called you to do for me.

You don't need anyone to help you, because I am with you and I am very happy that you listened to me to go down to the car dealership. You and Dorthula are very humble people. You have great things to do for me. Travel is on the way. When they invite you, only preach the truth. Don't have any fear, because I will be there with you always when you are preaching the truth of me (Jesus). Reverend Mildred is afraid of you because instead of helping you when you were sick, she always ran from you. Emmanuel wants to see you.

But don't set your heels on that place anymore. They do not have any good thoughts about you, that I (Jesus) am using you to do his work. Thus, they are causing jealousy, because they were not expecting you to come back to life. What they were expecting is that one day you would die, but rather they would die before you.

You have a work to do for me, and that is why I spared your life. Continue to love. Love your grandchildren in Africa. I put that love to you. They need you very much. It is true that your grandchildren prayed for your recovery and I restored you.

Don't you see how much Austin loves Dorthula? He is always calling Dorthula. That's the love the utile boy has for Dorthula.

The day sister jones came for a visit; she was surprised at what she saw. That is why she doesn't call frequently any more. She is a good woman. She loves the Lord. Her husband would live for a long time. New covenant holiness church is in shambles. No leader there. They are funny people. Someone who does not know you would say to you that you know everything about the church, and that is not true. Many things are going on in the church. The leader of the church has not come in as of yet. I will appoint the leader of the church to be a woman, not a man.

John is very proud about Sam. How God has promoted very high in the spirit. I have a special blessing for john if only he listens to my instructions. He must study Sam's life as an example. Sam is a quiet person, but not concerning the word (bible). My father has blessed Sam so much because he loves the Lord. Joseph would die in shame, because he always wants to see people's downfall. See what he did to Sam in his own church, reading the bible to disgrace Sam. Sam is now well. They are all jealous about you. Don't even drink water in their house.

Jeremiah 7:16

# Super Sunday—January 25th

**5:30 A.M. BEFORE SUNRISE**

My presence would be here today in apt 15e. I am bringing in the people to teach them my word, the gospel of our Lord Jesus Christ. The churches across doing nothing to promote me. Rather their mind is on money every time they meet. People are dying for the word. Most of them I have not called to work for me because they are using supernatural powers to work for me, which is of the devil. They will account for their doings when they die. The whole world is corrupt. My father is not happy with the world he created. There are too many thieves, robbers and murderers, because the churches are not doing their work. The only thing on their mind is the title of bishop, archbishop and pastor. In the kingdom there is no title. The work you do in this world will be judged by me, especially the so-called ministers. There is too much fornication and adultery in the churches than in past ages.

No one respects my father, who is in heaven and created the universe. Everyone will pay the price for the work they do for me. I came to the world because I love the world my father created. John 3:16: now no one regards my death on the cross. My mother and many are still crying for me, but she is at a better place where all the disciples are with me. Apostle Paul is the leader of them all. Acts 9: 1-22: Paul did a good job when I left the world. Sam is going to do much more for me. Dorthula should have patience with Sam. What is happening to him now in his life? And he still does not understand it, but I am the one who chose him. I am very proud of what he is doing for me. I gave you, Sam, the authority to use my name for bible studies. He is going to perform wonders in the years ahead.

The car is a reward for me, Sam and Dorthula. This is the second time that I am mentioning to Sam that he has suffered so much for my sake. His life was able to stand strong, but the safety was from heaven, I gave him more blessings to do my work. It is not a small job. The souls are in Satan's world. He cannot do it unless I prepare him to do it, and he is doing very well. I am around at all times. You cannot see me because I am a spirit. Sam, all those who belong to the Lord's bible studies will stay. Sam is learning very well. When the spirit leaves his body, Sam is a good man. Therefore, there is a reward for him. Sam has a good heart, and that's why I chose him to do my job after eleven years.

## Monday—February 2, 2015

The Lord's blessing is upon miracle of God. I am among you at the Holy Communion services. You, Sam, did everything well. That is the reason why I called you to stand for me. You are truly a man of God representing me in the way I want someone to represent me. I know who I have called to do my work. As I said earlier, all heaven and earth shall pass away, but my words would stand forever. It is the word that my father used to create the world. I, myself, am the word. Many people do not believe that I have come back to the world again. I am here in the spirit watching those so-called ministers cheating the people I have given to them. Their reward is waiting for them in hell, because I did not call them to use my name to make money, but rather to preach and win souls for the kingdom. Some of the ministers would die in shame. They have already had their reward here on earth. What are they expecting from me? Their wealth is nothing in the kingdom of God. Heaven is not a place for everyone. Unless you are holy you cannot enter the kingdom. It is not for fooling around. Everyone has work to do in the kingdom of God. No slacking in the kingdom.

Every person there works 24 hours a day.

My father is the light of the world. I said I would be coming again. And yes, the time is near. Everyone should prepare. No favor. That is why in my ministry on earth my first sermon that I, Jesus, preached was repentance. St. Mark

1:15: the time is fulfilled, and the kingdom of God is at hand; repent ye, and believe the gospel.

People do not want to submit themselves to me because they know I would have complete control over them. Yes, it is true. I created them in my own image and gave them life. Where are they running to now? I am everywhere at all times. People should learn a lesson from the woman at Jacob's well. That was an example to the world that Jesus came for everyone. In those days the Jews had no dealings with the Samaritans. Jesus asked her a simple question, "Give me to drink (water)." St. John 4:7-28: there cometh a woman of Samaria to draw water; Jesus sayeth unto her, "give me to drink."

Jesus then asked her to go and call her husband, because I cannot bless anyone without a husband. It is important for every believer to live a holy life. I will only bless those that are genuine, because they are precious in my sight.

Psalms 77:1-20: I cried unto God with my voice, even unto God with my voice, and he gave earth unto me.

There is only corruption in the world today. Everyone is doing their own thing, the things of the flesh. Someone is watching from above.

I am using Sam to preach the word. It is a gift of anointing from above. I have blessed you, Sam, with wisdom, knowledge and understanding to preach my word. A lot of churches will invite you to preach, but you are very serious to go to Germany. You will go there to preach the word.

Revelation 22:19: and if any man shall take away from the words of the book of this prophecy, God shall take away his part out of the book of life, and out of the holy city, and from the things which are written in this book.

The Holy Communion is very good. Now you are seeing the ones that are truly saved.

Many do not like Sam's preaching, because Sam would tell you exactly what the bible says with no subtraction or addition.

No one believes that I am with you, Sam. You have a lot to do concerning the gospel. I stood with you, Sam, at Augusta, Georgia, at the wedding, and ever since that day you have been writing. If Sam sleeps how can I speak with him? There are 24 hours in a day. Sam has enough time to sleep. He is doing two hours sleep, which covers his entire night.

I need people to do my work and Sam has been selected by numbers of angels to do the work.

Chronicles 16:27:

Glory and honor are in his presence; strength and gladness are in his place. Philippians 4:4: rejoice in the Lord always and again I say rejoice.

St. John 1:14: and the word was made flesh, and dwelt among us, and we beheld his glory, the glory as of the only begotten of the father, full of grace and truth.

I have to leave now.

Goodbye Sam,

*Jesus of Nazareth*

Sam is now a changed person. I did that during his sickness. Don't you see, Sam is not tired, because I am not tired in the kingdom? The word is everything in the kingdom. That is why I called him to preach hard to people, for them to change their lifestyle. Don't you see a lot of miracles Sam is doing? It's me, Jesus, doing the job through him. Everywhere he goes people will hear his name in the world, because I am going to do it at my own time.

Every member of "the Lord's bible studies" is blessed, and I will pour out my spirit upon them. I talk to Sam in the bathroom, because he is there alone and there is no one else to hear my voice. He is a chosen one from God to do my work. Miracles will be passing through him in the near future.

Revelation 3:20-21: behold, I stand at the door and knock; if any man hear my voice and open the door, I will come in to him, and will sup with him, and he with me.

Do the job, fear nobody. They cannot harm you. I am with you. Sam, be strong in the Lord and the power of his might. Because he refuses to work with you, I caused the sickness upon him. He does not listen to anyone; therefore he cannot do the work for me.

I will come again.

Keep up the good work I have given you to do.

Do you remember the wedding at Canaan? My presence changed everyone that was present. Marriage was instituted in the Garden of Eden. It is important for every man to marry. Marriage is holy in the sight of God.

In today's world, human beings have corrupted the universe so much. As it as it was in the days of Noah, so shall it be today. My father asked him to build an ark, and many people were laughing at him. But in the end what happened to them? They were all destroyed by the flood waters.

The time is coming very soon. In the near future the world must be changed to a new one. People would be surprised how things changed, but I had already told you, I will come again like a thief in the night at your door, and then if you are not ready you will go to hell. Better get ready, people, and be prepared for the coming of the Lord.

If repentance was not necessary, then why would I preach about it? Remember the prodigal son? St. Luke 15:13-31:

That is what my father is expecting the world to do, come to repentance. The world has become wayward because of technology. Too much time is spent on this, but who gave them the wisdom to do all things? My father, who has given them the knowledge and they forget him. Now they are making tons of money instead of helping the homeless people who are suffering in the world. Now, because of the Garden of Eden, Adam and eve refuse the lawful command my father gave them. He, Jesus, will not change the world now. It will only get worse.

Sam, I have prepared you for this work. You are doing a good job. It is a very difficult work, but you are trying your best. For every message you preach, I am with you. You are a faithful person. Sam loves people, but not those who do not love me, Jesus.

See what happened when Sam met the man at the supermarket. He was a man who believes in voodoo. I was right there in the spirit when Sam spoke with him. He will suffer in the world before he dies. He said that I, Jesus, is dead, but he would rather die in shame. He is going around fooling people, but my father will punish him. The cashier accepted the Lord because 0f what happened early that Sunday morning. I was right there when Sam defended me, that I am not dead, I am still alive. That is why I called Sam to do my work I left behind. He will do greater things in my name.

# Thursday—February 5, 2015

Sam, I want you to write. You always listen to me. You are such a blessing to me for my work to go on in this satanic world. Many people are suffering in the world because the devil is the one ruling the world today. It is very sad for people to listen to him. He has nothing to offer, only death. People better look for me. St. John 14:6; St. John 4:24; proverbs 21:15-30; Isaiah 43:10.

Goods friends, Richardson Thompson and Ethan, are your only good friends. Where are the others? They are all jealous about your gift, because they do not live a holy life. I do not dwell in a dirty house filled with flesh. I am a spirit, not a human being. How can I dwell in a dirty heart? Apt. 15e is clean and neat. I love this place. Dorthula, thank you for cleaning up every day. Thanks be to your mother, Rosie, for teaching you good things before she died.

The shining star is the star of heaven revealed to me, Sam, at 9:53 a.m.

Thomas will die. Do not feel pity for him. He did you wrong. Michael is also sick. They call me, Sam, to disgrace you in front of people. Sam, you are so blessed in many ways. You led me to the computer that morning to make the call and also make preparations to go to the holy land. This is what we call a blessing from the Holy Spirit.

Bye, bye,

*Jesus of Nazareth*

*Friday—February 6, 2015*

## OUT OF THE DARKNESS

When you enter into a dark room what do you do? Don't you put on the light to see things? I am the light of the world, and I came to prove that the world depends on the light of the universe to shine upon all people in the world. I am the light of the world and no other substance can change that. I came to loosen people from the bondage of the devil. Adultery, fornication and sexuality are the number one priority in the world, but the churches are the worse. Some of the pastors who are not called by me are all using supernatural powers in the churches to get more members without caring for souls. Church is a building in which people come to worship me in spirit and in truth.

Sam is a good person, but he does not take nonsense from anyone when he is preaching and teaching the word. Don't you know the word is life? St. John 6:63-65. I came to the world to win souls for the kingdom of God. Matthew 6:33-34; Isaiah 45:1-10. Once more I say repent and follow me. Mark 1:15. I said come unto me. Matthew 11:25-26.

People refuse to come to me because of their evil ways. You cannot hide from God. Psalms 139:7-10. Adam and eve hid from me, but they heard me when I called Adam. Your first parents Adam and eve brought this suffering in to the world, but today I send my son to come to remind people that I am still the God of Abraham, Isaac and Jacob, the God of the Jews and the gentiles. I am alpha and omega, the first and the last. My son, Jesus, has done a lot to save mankind. Why are people running from the creator? I am always in the world, which I created from nothing.

He went as far as to the cross to shed his blood for all mankind. He is still calling people to come to him.

St. John 14:6. I am the way, the truth and the life.

St. John 15: 1-14: this is the commandment that you should love one another, as I love you and laid down my life for you.

Isaiah 53:4-5.

St. John 14:10-12

## Friday—February 7, 2015

**HUMBLE YOURSELF UNTO GOD.**

I am the one doing the work in you. Sam, do not boast, but be humble as you always are. Bishop Johnson would suffer because he doesn't treat you well, but you were patient. That's why I promoted you. The car belongs to you. Keep your eyes on it. Try to visit the car every day. More blessings are coming to you. Sunday services, so far, are very good. You are doing well. I am always here during Holy Communion. Be careful about some suggestions. I call you and you alone. You can listen to any advice, but pray first and I will advise you whether it is good or not.

Arlene nearly collapsed when she saw you at the store. I don't believe she has completely made up her mind to come back to the Lord's bible studies. I am the son of God, but it doesn't mean I know everything. I am interceding for people in the world. I have already come back into this satanic world. Sam, you may soon see me in your dreams. Don't be afraid. I will direct you what to do when I send you to preach me (Jesus). She refuses to listen to you. I listen to my father always. That what we call respect. Don't you see how humble he was to the end? You are a good person, Sam, but many people don't know. Dorthula should thank her stars that she married you in 1987. Came to that apartment at St. Nicholas Avenue.

Pastor Sophia would die because she believes in the moon rather than me, the owner of life. How can you worship God and man? I am the light of the world. I can cause darkness. I just like that. Just don't sleep. Those who don't know will go to hell. Sam, let them know about heaven and hell. Don't worry about anything. The car is enough. I give you the car as a reward of your faithfulness and even the courage of preaching me always.

John is very proud of you, Sam. He doesn't talk to people just because he knows me. I (Jesus) called those my father has given to me. Sam is a good man. He is very strict in his life. He does not fool around in the world with my word.

There is a river flowing in this apartment. See, all the blessings for the Ahulu family and all those who belong to the Lord's bible studies. I gave you the name Sam for the Lord's bible studies. The trip will be a great reward for Sam for his faithfulness during sickness. Sam suffered but one thing. He kept the faith in me, Jesus. Sam needs courage to do the Lord's work. He is always dealing with the devil, but he always comes out victorious, because I, Jesus, have overcome the devil. He is real. Don't judge him wrong. Sam, don't sleep. Write. St. John 10:11-12. I am the good shepherd.

If you love me, keep my commandments. Love your neighbor as yourself.

I glorify you this morning. Glory hallelujah. I am the first and the last. Psalms 102. Revelation 20:1-8; psalms 110. Friday, Jesus speaks.

Bye, bye to Sam.

*Wednesday—February 11, 2015*

## I WOULD DEFINITELY COME BACK AGAIN. MY FATHER SAID SO.

St. John 1:1-30: john the Baptist did a good job. When he was in the world, he preached repentance of sins, and I preach repentance because the kingdom of God is at hand through me, Jesus.

Mark 1:15

Isaiah 23:1-15:

People must repent and accept me as Lord and savior, and also keep my commandments holy. Thou shall love the Lord thy God with all your heart, mind and soul, and keep my commandments holy.

Matthew 7:13-14: the narrow path to heaven. Sam, I have given you the wisdom to do the work for me in this world. The bible was given to mankind by my father; that is the power to us Christians. Those who wrote the bible did not know what they were writing. It was the Holy Spirit who interceded on their behalf to write what they wrote. Only the word that I preach would lead anyone who wants to enter into the kingdom. In heaven there will be only praise and worship, continually day and night. Only faithful and honest Christians will be there because of what I, Jesus, did on the cross to wash their sins away. I paid all your debts when I went to the cross. The only way to the kingdom of God is through me. St. John 14:6.

I called Sam to do my work. Even I, Jesus, find it difficult at times. That is why I called my disciples to help me pray in the garden of gethsemane. Dying on the cross seems like nothing, because it was already prophesied seven hundred years ago by the prophet Isaiah. My father already prepared me for this; it is very scary when you are in the flesh to think about what has been prophesied before.

Isaiah 53:4-5. My father gave me the victory; I could not have done it on my own.

The whole world will be judged. Therefore, Christians should live a holy life pleasing unto God. My father will not accept any excuses from sinners, because that is why my father sent me into this world to save sinners. Romans 3:23.

## Thursday—February 12, 2015

Matthew 11:25-30: at that time Jesus answered and said, I thank thee, o father, Lord of heaven and earth, because thou hast hid these things from the wise and prudent, and hast revealed them unto babes.

Revelation 22:1-10: and he showed me a pure river of water of life, clear as crystal, proceeding out of the throne of God and of the lamb.

St. John 14:6-23: Jesus sayeth unto him, I am the way, the truth, and the life. No man cometh unto the father but by me. If ye had known me, ye should have known my father also, and from henceforth ye know him and have seen him.

Romans 12:1-15: I beseech you, therefore, brethren, by the mercies of God, that ye present your bodies as a living sacrifice, holy, acceptable unto God, which is your reasonable service.

Exodus 20:1-10: and God spake all these words, saying, I am the Lord thy God, which have brought thee out of the land of Egypt, out of the house of bondage. Thou shalt have no other Gods before me.

Genesis 7:1-25: and the Lord said unto Noah, come thou and all thy house into the ark; for thee have I seen righteous before me in this generation.

Acts 1:8-13: but ye shall receive power. After that the Holy Ghost comes upon you, and ye shall be witnesses unto me, both in Jerusalem and Judaea, and in Samaria, and unto the uttermost part of the earth.

So far you are doing well, Sam. I am your protector. Pray and read the word.

Tell Cameron about himself and also the church. He, himself, is dealing in occult and also supernatural powers. He worships God and man. That is why I brought him down. He is not a good person. He is proud and arrogant, and also a womanizer. I have helped him a lot financially, but he spends most of his money on women. Judy made a fool of him. She loves money. At present she is not fine. She does not belong to any particular church.

Lloyd is not a good woman. She is a cheater and a liar, and pretends she loves her husband, but she treats him like a little boy.

Kim will end badly. How can she belong to "the Lord's bible studies" with filthiness in her heart? She has been living in the flesh for many years. She also dominates the man, and she cannot praise me, Jesus, living in such a life.

Deaconess Conwall is a very worried woman, because her mother does not like Steven. But she went ahead anyway and married him. She was very young when she married Steven, her husband. He is a very lazy person. He does not like to do hard jobs. He refuses to take advice from anyone, even me, Jesus. His end will not be better unless he changes his manners.

I brought him to you and Dorthula because of transportation. Don't you see, you are no closer? I have now given you a beautiful car. You do not need his assistance now. He refuses to obey what I said about water baptism. How can you enter heaven without being water baptized? It is very important, the washing away of your sins. St. John 1:26-27.

Dorthula's family is in shock. They did not know that this calling from the Lord was upon Sam. This is what we call a blessing from the Lord. Deut. 28: 1-15. No one can understand it. Sam suffered so much for this kind of blessing. I called Sam a long time ago in 1975 while he was in the navy. He suffered severe sickness. At that time he was very young, about 35 years old. I brought him to the United States to be ordained as a full minister. There the temptations started, but he did well to stand for it. Sam is a very faithful person. I love him very much, especially the way he represents me, Jesus, when he is preaching the word. He is a very powerful man. He is still very strong. Sam is very rich spiritually.

## Thursday—February 12, 2015

St. John 14:6: I am the way, the truth and the life; no one cometh unto the father, but by me. I am using Sam to prove to the world when he goes to the world conference to let people know that I am still alive and in the world. Sam is very clever. He really knows the word, which is the bible. He loves God so much and does not take nonsense when he is around people who speak negatively about God. It would be trouble, because he is full of the Holy Spirit from above.

I chose him to work for me because he loves and fears God in his heart. He always responds to me, Jesus, when I call upon him. Dorthula helps Sam do the work I have called him to do.

God chose Sam because he loves people, and he will be travelling all over the world to preach for me. Sam is a good person to do the preaching. He likes to proclaim the word of God wherever he goes, but people are still planning to kill him, however they cannot, because I am with him wherever he goes. It is all about jealousy and his anointing from heaven. Sam suffered for this blessing for eleven years. Sam is in the world, but not really here from September 2003 through September 2014. I gave him the victory over his enemies. Some people who judge him wrongly died, and some are now sick, but Sam repented and forgave them. That is what we call repentance. The first ministry john reached about was repentance, but I preach about the Holy

Ghost; Sam now has the Holy Ghost's power to preach the good news of me anytime, because I have given him wisdom about the word. I need people to work for me, but unless they are holy as I am a spirit, they will not be able to do my work.

We cannot work for God in the flesh, because in the kingdom it is only the Holy Spirit and all the angels who travel everywhere in the world to do my work.

The trip would be great. The whole world would be coming to the holy land to see what I established on earth.

The Garden of Eden is still operating in the middle of Africa where the tree of life is.

I gave the name "the Lord's bible studies" to the organization. Sam is very good in teaching about the Holy Communion. That is the way I like it to be done. I asked him to use Isaiah 53:4-5. Nobody can criticize him. I gave him that authority to use it. Don't you see the difference in it? People still doubt Sam. Sam is a prophet in my sight, because he himself does not know.

## Friday—February 13 2015

Sam, I am always with you. This is the beginning of your work. You have a lot more to do for me. It is about time for me to leave this house and go to the highways. At apartment 15e all the angels love there because only Jesus is in this house. Be prepared for this work assignment.

Bye, bye for now,

*Jesus of Nazareth*

## Friday—February 13, 2015

Sam, I am here at this moment. I am listening to your prayers. So far you are doing very well. Continue the good work I have called you to do for me. Your brother-in-law is very shocked about his daughter coming to know the Lord.

It is not you of yourself who did that miracle. I am the one, Jesus, doing it through you. So far you are doing well.

What is Valentine's Day? The love I have given to the world is more than that of Valentine's Day. It is better for people to have the love of God in their hearts, but no one cares about God's love anymore.

St. John 3:16-17: for God so loved the world that he gave his only begotten son, that whosoever believeth in him should not perish, but have everlasting life. For God sent not his son into the world to condemn the world; but that world through him might be saved.

People are refusing me everyday to live in sin and do the worldly things of this satanic world. They think they will live forever, but that is impossible. Once you are born into this world, you must die. Hebrews 9:27.

Amos 4:12: therefore, thus will I do unto thee, o Israel, and because I will do this unto thee, prepare to meet thy God.

I, Jesus, started my mission on earth preaching "repentance." St. Mark 1:15: repent ye, and believe the gospel. People still do not care about the things which are of God; they have taken God completely out of their lives.

Wives and husbands are made number one, first priority in their lives instead of God, the creator. There is a day coming when everyone will stand for themselves.

2 Corinthians s: 10: for we must all appear before the judgment seat of Christ; that every one may receive the things done in his body according to that he hath done, whether it be good or bad.

No one will be excused on that Day of Judgment, and only true Christians who obey my words and keep my commandments.

Exodus 20:3-17: thou shalt have no other gods before me.

People are all corrupt and have no happiness in their homes. I, Jesus, revealeth to you, Sam, and your friend in the car, the real meaning of the Garden of Eden and the forbidden tree of life that covers the whole world. That is the reason why my father is so angry about our first parents.

The human race should have been blessed more than this, but eve caused the damaged between the relationship with God and the world.

Sam, do not listen to anybody except me, Jesus. I called you personally to continue my work I left behind. The so-called pastors are playing with their lives. They think I am with them, but I am not. The devil is working in their churches. They are not of me.

The worst people in the world today are the ministers. They are worse than thieves in the prisons. I will punish them when they die, because they are putting shame on me, and the devil is laughing all the time because of their behavior. The whole world is corrupt and people are taking sex as a joke. This is a very sacred act between couples. People are selling their bodies for money, especially the young ones between the ages of 10-13 years.

Technology has taken over the whole world instead of God. Technology is being worshipped by people all over the world.

Matthew 16:26: for what is a man profited if he shall gain the whole world and lose his own soul? Or what shall a man give in exchange for his soul?

I will be there for Holy Communion on Sunday.

I have put in your heart to give the certificate to mother sally. I chose her so she would spread the news about "the Lord's bible studies."

Sam, people say you know all that is going on, but how can you know if I do not revel things to you. Some of them are already jealous about you and the car I gave to you. And Dorthula, the time you were suffering no one cares. They were enjoying themselves. Now, see the blessings are coming.

Dorthula should be very careful around her own people. They pretend a lot. Stephanie was taken by me, Jesus. She was not happy in the world. She was created beautiful like her mother. She conducted herself well in this satanic world.

Heaven is a good place to live, but unless you are holy you cannot enter. I am the only one who has the authority to open the big gates.

St. John 14:6: Jesus sayeth unto him, I am the way, the truth and the life. No man cometh unto the father but by me.

My father is a good God to the world, Sam. I will be back.

Continue the way you are going. I am proud of you. Tell Dorthula to understand you.

It is the anointing upon you, and that is why you're acting like that.

St. John 3:8-12: the wind bloweth where it listeth

And. Thou hearest the sound thereof, but canst not tell whence it cometh and wither it goeth so is every one that is born of the.

Bye, bye for now,

*Jesus of Nazareth*

# Sunday—February 15, 2015

**12:30 A.M.**

Why do you doubt your calling? Sam, you suffered so much for this. Why are you not happy? I will protect you wherever you go. No one can harm you. You are chosen to do the work of an evangelist not a pastor. There are a lot of temptations, especially the women in the churches. They commit adultery and make sexual advances toward the ministers, and if you are not strong spiritually you would be compelled to do the things you do not want to do. The devil brings the churches down. Therefore, Sam, be very careful. The temptations will come in different forms, but I am with you always. Just concentrate on the word and everything will be fine. You are going to perform a lot of miracles in my name.

I have never called rev. Bryce to do a work for me. Also, rev. Courtney is sick. The church is not doing anything to promote me; rather they focus on money and people's properties instead of coming together and praying hard.

You would go on a world tour in the years ahead. People would be following you around, but be just friends to them.

I gave the car to Sam because of Dorthula. She is always accusing Sam of not having a car. I asked him in the spirit form for Dorthula to choose the car so she would stop worrying. I caused Mr. Gilbert to do what he did so you would get the car. I was there that Saturday when they handed the car to Sam. I also caused him not to ask a lot of questions, otherwise Sam would not get the car. And yes, I am always around the car I gave to Sam so he can use it for my work.

I would be present for Holy Communion in the spirit. Good bye, Jesus of Nazareth

Sam, your prayers have been heard. Pray every morning at six o'clock. More blessings are coming from the Lord.

## Tuesday—February 17, 2015

Sam, you see what I have done for you and Dorthula again in your life. I opened her heart to contribute to the organization, because I know what is going to happen one day. I would be going with you. You will be called to testify of your life and also to tell of the miracles that I am performing in your life. Many churches would like you to preach, but I will advise you where to go. Not all of them are preaching the truth. They are making cover-ups. You cannot preach in those churches. There is going to be a very big occasion.

I talked to your heart this morning to go to the computer, and I directed you what to do in the spirit. A lot of people from all over the world will be attending; people from Russia, Germany, Australia, Amsterdam, New Zealand, Scotland, England, Sweden, South Africa, Jamaica, Italy, Greece and the United States of America. You will be well known in the world because of me. Do not boast, because I am the one doing the work through you. You are a completely changed person. Dorthula does not understand you, because the blessing comes so fast. The time you were suffering no one cared, but now everyone is jealous of you.

Sam, you are in the spiritual world. You understand everything I am telling you to do. That is the only way to enter into the kingdom of God by holiness and the gospel which you preach.

I am going to do many wonderful things with you. Eleven years is a long time for your sickness. I did that for you to know there is something in this world like supernatural powers from heaven. There is no difference between you and the apostle Paul. It is the same call from me. My father and your father are very happy for you, Sam and Dorthula. You both have suffered so much, especially you, Sam, with that spiritual sickness. You died half way to your grave, but you kept the faith in me.

Sam, continue playing the gospel music. Angels are there all the time listening to the music. Morning and evening they are there, but because they are spirit you cannot see them. They observe everything you are doing.

Summer will be very busy for you, but I will be going with you wherever you go. Many people will receive me and be baptized in me. The young man you met some time ago is an angel, but you did not know and you offered to help him.

Do not worry about money, rather the word of God that is more important. Don't you see everywhere you go people like you? It is because of the light that is upon you. Dorthula is a bit jealous of you, but you do not have time for women. All I want you to do now is to preach the word everywhere you go on the streets. I do not hesitate to talk through you anywhere in the world.

Sam has no time for anything except the word (bible). He is just like Paul in the bible no one can stand in front of him concerning the word. Sam is very smart. One thing with him is that he is very humble. He never boasts 0f his calling. It is a special call from above. More blessings are coming. The car is nothing.

Sam, be careful about men. They would like to destroy you, but they can't because there has been a light around you since September 2014, and it is going to be with you and Dorthula forever.

Dorthula will have visions in the future. Don't spend too much money buying things. You will have enough to wear everyday.

Ministers are not doing a good job. Some started out good, but are now corrupt because of the love of money. Some ministers should listen to God rather than to their wives. They are all thinking of ways to make money, and then they forget about me. I have already blessed them, but they forget. They will all die and meet me.

Matthew 7:21: not everyone that sayeth unto me Lord, Lord shall enter into the kingdom of heaven; but he that doeth the will of my father which is in heaven.

Sam, always quote this scripture, because it is a very serious chapter in the bible. For the so called ministers. A lot of them I have never called; they called themselves. How can I accept them in the kingdom if they are not holy? They would rather live in the flesh and be with the women in the churches.

That's why I asked Sam not to be involved in a church any longer.

Sam obeyed my word. That is why I love him so much. His calling is a very special calling.

Keep it up. Going now.

Bye, I will be back again. Bye for now.

This house is blessed. I like the Holy Communion. Sam is very serious about God now more than then.

Leave him alone. It is the spirit upon him, and it is very powerful.

## Tuesday—February 17, 2015

Be prepared for this work. Sam, greater works I have waiting for you in the holy land, and I am going to be there with you to perform miracles, especially in your preaching. I have prepared you to do this work. Your sickness has brought you great blessings from heaven.

I like the way you represent me in the public places and on the street. That is why I love you. I have called you since 1975 in Africa, but you did not understand my calling at that time. The word of God is everything in this world, and I did it for you, Sam, in bringing back everything to your memory. You are the only person having such knowledge of the word in the modern world. Sam is going to perform miracles in the future in my name.

I will open the doors for you in the holy land of my birth. When you go take pictures everywhere and show the people.

The narrow path is the best way to walk, but the broad way leads to destruction. On the narrow path you experience hatred, persecution and false accusations, but keep your faith in me. Nobody can harm you, Sam. I am always with you in the spirit.

I, Jesus, gave Sam the scriptures to back his preaching and teachings. His request has been granted to preach the word everywhere he goes. It is an open door for Sam. The world will know him as a prophet.

I say Isaac and Ishmael are brothers. They should sit down and settle their differences. War cannot solve their problems; it going to take mutual understanding to come to an agreement. Peace will not come to Israel unless both sides agree on common grounds. Both are brothers from the womb spiritually.

Patience can move mountains. Moses did very well to control the Israelites. They are very stubborn. Even up to this day they would always suffer, because they reject their own. God is watching. Can't they sit down and talk? The soul that sins shall die. Ezekiel 19:1-20

A father will not stand for a child, neither the son; each and every one will stand for their own sins. You all better confess your sins to me and have life.

Proverbs 28:13: he that covereth his sins shall not prosper, but who so confesseth and forsaketh them shall have mercy.

Proverbs 22:2: the rich and the poor meet together. The Lord is the maker of them all. There is a lot going on in the world and I can't wait for my father to let me come and rule the whole world with iron hands to correct things in this satanic world. This world was created beautifully by my father, and human beings have destroyed it. He gave the Garden of Eden to Adam and eve. They disobeyed the commandment of God by allowing the devil to deceive them. That's why the world is suffering today. Things will be restored when I come back in the flesh. Now I am here in the spirit and I am watching everything going on in the world. It is better to follow Abraham in faith when my father called him.

Genesis 12: 1-7: Abraham is still alive in the kingdom. Moses, Joshua, Elijah and other prophets are all there. The whole world is also suffering because of what happened generations ago. It is better to listen and do the commandment of God than to take the world for granted.

One day my father and your father will strike as in the days of Noah. Do not take it as a joke; it is going to happen. The father is watching them carefully and technology will disappear completely, as this is one reason why the world is in such turmoil.

In the world my father created there was no light, and he spoke and there was great light in the world. My father loves the world he created. St. John 3:16.

## Wednesday—February 18, 2015

How can you tell people their future and you are not a prophet. I, Jesus, say that you are a prophet. Sam, you are too humble. Wake up and speak the word (bible). I have already given you the wisdom for the word. Do not listen to anybody in the family, as most of them do not speak the truth. Yes, it is true that the rich man is doing something for Matthews in Atlanta, Georgia. She is just fooling around. Her life is in danger, but she does not know. She also does not have any respect for anyone. The only things on her mind are to do lots of big things in life, but today where is the business she said she was going to start? It is all garbage and nothing ever comes through for her.

There is a lot of jealousy in this family. People think they know much more about God, but they do not. You just wait and see what happens in the future. Diddy, is the worst. That boy respects no one. Pride has filled him up. He will definitely fall. Watch and see his end from me, Jesus. How can you stop people from coming to learn and know about God? He is a devil in disguise. Bell is not a happy person at all. She pretends a lot. She is a bit astonished that her father did not die.

Sam does not take nonsense from anyone.

The children are so happy about their grandparents. They see everything that is going on around them, especially Bryce.

Ellen's husband regrets he married her, but it is too late now because she is like a snake in the grass.

Sam, do not worry about anything. Minster Stanley needs help spiritually in his mind. The wife's sickness is affecting him dearly. Sam, try to help him. He loves you very much. He is not qualified to work with you. You need a very strong person like you to work with. I prayed through Bernie that he will know that you are not playing in apartment 15e, but that you are working for me, Jesus.

Sam has suffered so much in life, but still he has the faith in me, Jesus. That is why Sam is here today. He likes to help people who are in need, not for show. He does it from his heart and he does not boast. That is why I love him. He is also very quiet in nature, but do not fool around him with God. Then you will see his behavior. Everybody loves him because he has a good heart. Dorthula should study Sam very well. He has a clean heart. Don't you see it?

All Sam wants is to preach the word about me, Jesus, and nothing else. He is truly a man of God equipped with the gospel.

Sam loves God and my father. I have to leave now. Until next time. Bye, bye. Jesus. End.

## Thursday—February 19, 2015

Sam, all your enemies would die before you. They envy you because of the scriptures I give you. I have given the wisdom to know the bible and to preach the truth. Dorthula is there to help you. Don't let anybody help you with the work I have given you to do. Don't have fears within you and do not entertain fears. Joshua 1:8-9. You are just like them. I have finished for the day.

Jesus of Nazareth

Keep up the good work. Dorthula, be happy with Sam. Your blessings are coming because of Sam's faithfulness.

Bye, bye, Sam.

# Friday—February 20, 2015

**1:00 A.M.–2:55 A.M.**

Sam, I do not want you to sleep. I called you to work for me. Do not listen to anybody. You were sick alone. It is only by grace that you were healed. You were near death, walking only as a human being, but the spirit was almost gone out of you. Be happy that my father loves you. He is the one that brought you back. Be careful. Do not listen to people. They are not the ones who healed you. I am the one who brought you back to life.

The world is full of evil. Do not take any chances with your life again. The reason why I called you is to preach me, Jesus, to the world. I am still in the world, but only in the spirit. I have given Sam the wisdom and knowledge to preach the word and nothing else. Rev 22:19

Rev 22:15: the bible is the divine word given to mankind.

Your grandchildren in Ghana love you, Sam, very much. They are the ones who prayed for you not to die and I heard their prayers. One of your grandchildren is definitely going to be a minister. She is very clever in many ways. She is the spiritual force in the family. Before Sunday Holy Communion services, members should examine themselves carefully before partaking of the Holy Communion.

Sam is a holy man of God. He is going to be known all over the world. I preach not dance on the Sea of Galilee.

Mark 1:15–repentance.

Jesus said, "I am the light of the world, the alpha and the omega."

I pour out my blood to save lives, but yet still people do not believe that I am alive after being resurrected.

Sam, you are always in the spiritual world. That's why I love you so much. Salvation is of the Lord. Do not play with my angels for heaven to keep things going with me. It was john who baptized with water, but I baptize with the Holy Spirit.

People would ask how can I talk to you, but they do not know that you are always in the spirit and that you listen to me whenever I talk to you.

Eleven years of sickness is not a joke, but I have prepared you, Sam, for the job. There is going to be much more work for you to do for me. Do not sleep Sam. Wake up a person must sleep, but also must know that someone is keeping him.

The Lord's bible studies are blessed from heaven. I used john to encourage you, Sam, because that boy loves you as a father. John is very proud of you. He talks about you all the time. His God has promoted him very high in the spirit. I do have a special blessing for him, if only he keeps his mouth. He must study the life of you.

Sam is a good person; but concerning the word (bible), my father has blessed Sam so much because he loves my father.

Adam would die in shame because he always wants to see others' downfalls. See what he did to Sam. He tried to disgrace Sam in his own church. Now Sam is well. They are all jealous about his anointing. Do not even drink water in their house. Archbishop Albert would continue to suffer, because he buried me for a second time.

Be happy, Sam. I am with you. I am leaving now. I said be careful, Sam. Matt. 7:21-34. Not everyone that sayeth unto me shall enter into the kingdom of heaven, but he that doeth the will of my father, which is in heaven.

Acts 2:38-41: then peter said unto them, repent and be baptized every one of you in the name of Jesus Christ for the remission of sins, and ye shall receive the gift of the Holy Ghost.

If you love me, be my disciple.

Matt. 28:18-20. All power is given unto me in heaven and in earth. Go ye therefore and teach all nations, baptizing them in the name of the father, and of the son, and of the Holy Ghost. I called them to preach the gospel. Whatever you sow in this world, that shall ye also reap.

The ministers are killing me, Jesus, every day. They do not live the life as chosen people. They represent me as dogs without owners running around. I am watching everything that is going on in this world, and my eyes are not closed like a blind person.

I am the one speaking through my servant Sam. I have called him to continue to do the work that the apostle Paul left behind. I will bless him because he is faithful in doing my work. I will send you to go out to the world to preach the gospel. Matt. 28:18-20.

What are you siding down waiting for? Preach repentance, Sam, with you and your household. No one can do you any harm; my eyes are always upon you.

Do not think about death, you have already passed death. I will expose some people and put them to a big shame. It is coming very soon to them.

Do not stop going to the highways. Have patience with Dorthula. I will protect you. Continue to pray more daily. Don't you see the signs I have been doing in your prayer room? I am always there with you. Do not be afraid. More miracles are coming through you. Don't you see I provide you with a car?

I, Jesus, touched the heart of your wife not to leave you because of the sickness. I was preparing you to do the job for me. I need holy people. Yes, it was a long time, and all due to the preparation of the job. I do not want you to be in the flesh, but in spirit.

Mark 1:15. Preach repentance.

## Wednesday—February 18, 2015

St. John 14:6: Jesus sayeth unto him, I am the way, the truth and the life; no man cometh unto the father, but by me. I came that they must have life and have it more abundantly, but some refuse to accept Jesus. But at the end of the day they will all suffer in the fire of brimstone. I am still in the world, but people do not recognize me. They are all in the flesh and the flesh cannot inherit the kingdom of God. I am a spirit, and you must be born again to receive the spirit of God. St. John 3:8.

Nicodemus came to me to know about the kingdom. People should know that God is real in the kingdom. My father does not take any excuses in the kingdom. If you do not know me, you go to hell. I came to the world to prove there are a heaven and a hell, and mankind has no caring for me. They take advantage of the beautiful world I created. In the end they will see what is coming to this satanic world. This is not a joke. The devil is ruling the hearts of the people. There is fornication, adultery, no social justice in the court houses, man marrying man, and woman marrying woman. This is all like Sodom and Gomorrah. God is watching. People will suffer at the hands of God because they have no respect for God.

Everybody's mind is on making money. The day is coming very soon that they will know that I am alive in the world. Christians are not living the life as Christians. They are all destroying me. No one will escape the judgment, I and the one in charge. If you refuse me, I will also refuse in front of my father in heaven. Then where are you heading? To hell, of course. Let me tell you, hell is real. This is not a joke. When you die you will see the truth.

There is no division between black and white. Each and every one will face the judgment seat to confess their sins to my father. Proverbs 28:13; 1 john 1:9.

1st. John 14:6: Jesus sayeth unto him, I am the way, the truth, and the life; no man cometh unto the father, but by me.

## Wednesday—February 18, 2015

Sam saved most of the family members because I asked him to do so. Sam is doing a wonderful job for this family. Don't you see how he talks with authority? I gave him the power to be like that.

An Israel tour is the way to heaven on earth. Many people would invite you to speak in their churches. Do not panic. I am always with you in the spirit. Yes, you always refer to the Garden of Eden and eve. Yes, she is the reason why the whole world is suffering today. My father in not happy and the so-called ministers are making money using my name. Punishment is coming soon to some of them. Money, money that would never lead to the promised land, which is heaven.

No short cut.

St. John 14:6: I am the way, the truth, and the life; no man cometh unto the father, but by me.

Revelation 22:10-20: and he sayeth unto me, seal not the sayings of the prophecy of this book, for the time is at hand. He that is unjust, let him be unjust still; and he that is filthy, let him be filthy still; and he that is righteous, let him be righteous still; and he that is holy, let him be holy still.

Sam is the chosen one that I have called. He would never rest to do his work. Dorthula, help Sam to do something in the ministry. I am always with him. Dorthula, be careful how you talk to Sam. Sam always tells you that one day I will strike, and it is true. It will happen, but not you, Dorthula. Many things are happening in your family. Sam has no family here. All are deceased. Dorthula, just be careful and watch Sam carefully. He is always in the spirit. Don't you see he is always ready to preach?

Bishop Ahulu is nothing without the spirit. He is always in the spirit because he wants to work for the Lord. Salvation is from above, not from anyone.

Sam has been talking to celinesusan to come to prayer meeting, but she never comes. She is always giving excuses about her car being damaged. She was ashamed when she met Sam. All what Sam was telling her about me, Jesus, she thought was a joke, but now she has seen it manifest that Sam was speaking the truth about me.

This generation is so corrupt and wicked. No respect for anyone. This happens because of the parents they are without me. They think I will bless them, but I will not, because they do not know me. Sam, men do not like you because of your gift. Ricky will continue to suffer because he buried me for a second time. Where is Rev. Bruce Jones? He is gone and I am still here. I am the creator of all things.

I sent Sam that day to preach at rev. Francisco's church, but he was not there. Sam preached a very powerful message that day. When they invite you to come and preach in their church, do not do because they will kill you. But they can't because I am with you always. Just be careful.

It is getting late, and the sun will soon be appearing.

Bye, bye, Sam.

Good job.

# Thursday—February 19, 2015

**10:21 A.M.**

People need you, Sam, in their homes to pray for them, but be careful about that because the devil is busy. He wants to put you to shame, but don't worry, I will guide you wherever you go.

I am pleased with you. Not many preachers have what you have. It is a blessing from me, Jesus. You are the last apostle to do my work in the world. All the angels in heaven are rejoicing because of you. My Father is very happy about you and Dorthula. Dorthula's family is now wondering about you, and that at your age God has called you to do his work. They are shocked. Dorthula was a blessed woman. The very day she decided to marry you. I cause that marriage to happen, but how can someone marry a person who is sick? I performed that miracle because you, Sam, have a good name and Dorthula needs someone special as a true representative of the Almighty God.

Start preparations now for Israel. Time is running fast. A lot of angels will be there to witness the ceremony. This will be good for your and Dorthula to be there also, because of the anointing upon Sam.

The car is a miracle car. It would be hard for people to believe that I have called you and given it to you, but the Holy Spirit is telling you to go and claim it.

Because people are in darkness, they only see the things in the flesh, but if you are led by the spirit you will be able to follow the directions of Jesus Christ.

Matt. 16:26; For what is a man profited if he shall gain the whole world and lose his own soul? Or what shall a man give in exchange for his soul?

## Thursday—February 19, 2015

Hell is real. It is not a good place for anyone to go. I know it is not prepared for the human beings. The spirit is in torment. The devil is also real and will be locked away by my father for a thousand years. Have no doubt in your mind about that. The stories in the bible are true.

Moses was chosen to be a good leader for my people in Israel. Joshua did a very good job to lead my people, the Israelites, to the promised land, but now they are suffering because they do not believe in me, Jesus.

Your grandchildren in Africa are very proud of you and Dorthula.

Sam, do not worry about what they say about you. They did the same thing to me when I was here. That's the work of the devil. If you give yourself to the devil, he will definitely use you.

Mildred, pray more. Don't you see Sam loves to pray? That is his weapon to do the work I have chosen him to do. Without prayer how can you seek God's face? People forget God is a spirit.

St. John 4:24-26: God is a spirit, and they that worship him must worship him in spirit and in truth.

How can you see a spirit? I am always walking among you people, but you cannot see me, because you do not have spiritual eyes to see me.

I asked Sam to go to the computer that day. Sam does not know how to use the computer, but the Holy Spirit led him and a miracle happened. He was led by the spirit to find the Jerusalem prayer team. This is the place where people were rushing to make their bookings to go to Israel for the celebration of the heritage center, which was being opened for the first time.

Sam always listens to me. Had he not gone to the computer that time I spoke to him, this miracle would not have happened. Obedience is better that sacrifice. Joshua 1:8.

Reading the word is like Joshua to him, and that is what I am expecting from him and every believer. Your body is the temple of God. Keep it holy. God is holy, and there is no darkness around him. It is all spiritual.

The world is now on the verge of collapsing because there is too much evil in the world. Children do not respect their parents because of technology. This will all come to an end very soon.

Sunday communion is already in a good position to continue Isaiah 53:4-5.

Sam, there is great wickedness all over the world. Sam, prepare for a miracle. I am leaving now. Bye, bye. Jesus.

## Sunday—February 22, 2015

Sam, I am always with you. I called you to do my work for me. Do not mind what people say about you. They do not like you, but they cannot do you anything. The light is too much around you. Sam, you are very obedient and humble. That is why I love you. You do not boast; you are a very simple person. Everybody loves you. Even the angels in heaven are rejoicing about you. Sometimes I do not understand why you love me so much.

When you were a young boy, you refused to be baptized, because you did not know the real meaning of baptism and what it was all about. This is a very important path in someone's life. It is the only way to enter into the kingdom of God.

I want you, Sam, to go to the world conference center in Israel to let people know that I am still alive in the world today and forever.

Psalms 34:1-7: I will bless the Lord at all times; his praise shall continually be in my mouth. My soul shall make me boast in the Lord. The humble shall hear thereof, and be glad. 0, magnify the Lord with me, and let us exalt his name together. I sought the Lord, and he heard me, and delivered me from all my fears.

Isaiah 53:1-10: who hayeth believed our report? And to whom is the arm of the Lord revealed? He shall grow up before him as a tender plant, and as a root out of a dry ground; he hath no form nor comeliness; and when we shall see him there is no beauty that we should desire him.

Colossians 3:1-10: if ye then be risen with Christ, seek those things which are above, where Christ sits on the right hand of God. Set your affection on things above, not on things on the earth.

The world is very corrupt because of evil. I said again, St. Mark 8:36: for what shall it profit a man if he shall gain the whole world, and lose his own soul?

Matthew 6:36: but seek ye first the kingdom of God and his righteousness, and all other things shall be added unto you.

People should seek God first in their lives. The flesh profiteth nothing. You ought to be born again, not by the flesh, but by the spirit. There is no way we can worship God in the carnal mind. It has to be in the spirit, which is from God and God alone.

Moses did all that he could do for the children of Israel, but he did not get to the promised land because he did not listen to me. That is why I say again and again, Sam always listens when I speak to him. That is why I am blessing him. Dorthula, be happy and listen to Sam always. Sam is a very good person and everybody loves him. He has a few enemies because of his wisdom of the bible.

Dorthula, go and buy the yellow roses and put them in front of your daughter's picture in the living room. I said it and you heard when I spoke to you in the bedroom.

People cannot sleep and do my work. They have to wake up. Sleeping is like you are dead.

Lynn should be very careful about sam. I called him to help set a firm standing in that family. Was something wrong with that? Lynn should stop the gossiping and give good advice to other people.

People would say that Sam knows all things, but he does not know it. I am the one speaking through him to do the work.

Yes, Sam is a prophet. He can tell people their future, but sometimes he does not want to do it. See the case in Ghana? That is an example of prophecy. The sister was surprised about the prophecy being fulfilled about the churches that they are operating with the satanic powers, which is from the devil.

Ezekiel 37: 1-10: the h0 the Lord was upon me, and carried me out in the spirit of the Lord, and set me down in the midst of the valley, which was full of bones, and caused me to pass by them around and behold, there were very many in the open valley; and lo, they were very dry.

If my spirit is not there then I am not there.

Zechariah 4:6: then he answered and spake unto me, saying this is the word of the Lord unto zerubbabel, saying, not by might, nor by power, but by my spirit, sayeth the Lord of hosts.

(Sam, you are right. Only in the spirit can you do my work. You always minister about my baptism, and how my father sent the Holy Spirit upon me to start my ministry on earth.

St. Mark 1:15: and saying, the time is fulfilled and the kingdom of God is at hand; repent ye and believe the gospel.

Without repentance how can you see the kingdom of God?

Romans 12:1: I beseech you therefore brethren, by the mercies of God, that ye present your bodies as a living sacrifice, a holy acceptable unto God, which is your reasonable service.

Revelation 3:20: behold, I stand at the door, and knock; if any man hear my voice and open the door, I will come in to him, and will sup with him, and he with me.

I am always present with you, Sam, everywhere you go, and my light shines upon you always.

Exodus 32:1-12: and when the people saw that Moses delayed to come down out of the mount, the people gathered themselves together unto Aaron, and said unto him, "up, make us gods, which shall go before us; for as for this Moses, the man that brought us up out of the land of Egypt, we wot not what is become of him."

And Aaron said unto them, "Break off the golden earrings, which are in the ears of your wives, of your sons, and of your daughters, and bring them unto me."

When the people saw that Moses had delayed, they supposed that he had lost his way in the darkness or perished in the fire. The people gathered themselves together unto Aaron, the elder brother of Moses, and said unto him, "Until he, Moses, comes down, make us gods, which shall go before us." All the people broke off their gold and melted it down and made graven images.

Aaron made a proclamation and said that tomorrow would be the feast.

But the Lord said unto Moses, "Go, get thee down, and see they are worshipping graven images, which I have warned them against. I would reject and despite them of the privilege that had. Moses." Then he turned and went down from the mountain. Moses' anger was waxed a lot and cast the tables out of his hands and broke them beneath the mount.

Exodus 32:20: and he took the calf which they had made and burnt it in the fire, and ground it to powder, and strewed it upon the water, and made the children of Israel drink it.

Aaron said, "Let not my anger of my Lord be in the gates of the camp. He, Moses said, 'who is on the Lord's side come to me.'" the zeal and courage of Moses was astonishing, considering the opposition of the people. The people were separated into this division. Some of them were put to death, and the rest who withdrew in shame or sorrow were speechless.

Moses said to the people, "ye, have ye sinned a great sin?"

Exodus 32:32: yet now, if thou wilt forgive their sin, and if not, blot me, I pray thee, out of thy book which thou hast written, but Christ actually died for his people.

Romans 5:8: but God commendeth his love towards us in that while we were yet sinners, Christ died for us.

Moses prayed to God for the people, and God abandoned them of their sins.

The judgment is real and there is no joke about it. People; be prepared to meet thy God.

Amos 4:12: therefore, thus will I do unto thee, 0 Israel; and because I will do this unto thee, prepare to meet thy God, 0 Israel.

Read my word daily; believe and meditate upon it. God bless Sam and Dorthula.

Good bye,

*JESUS OF NAZARETH*

## Monday—February 23, 2015

**AFTER LORD'S SUPPER**

Sam, I was right there with you in your apartment. Everything went well and I am happy how you conducted the service. I will continue to bless you and entire family of "the Lord's bible studies." Uncle Robert really prayed through the Holy Spirit. Donna is not of herself because of the family matters. She should be concentrating on the Lord and forget about worldly things. Mother Dorothy was really surprised after I told you, Sam, to speak to her about her situation. Sam, you did exactly what I told you to do.

Sam has been set aside to teach and preach. Don't you see Sam is a changed person? I am the one working through him. He will perform more wonderful miracles in my name. You will see how much I will bless everyone in the end. I led Sam to revelation 22:1-2.

And he showed me a pure river of water of life, clear as a crystal, proceeding out of the throne of God and of the lamb. In the midst of the street of it, and on either side of the river, was there the tree of life, which bore twelve manners of fruits, and yielded her fruit every month; and the leaves of the tree were for the healing of the nations.

Dorthula did well in reading of my word. She is very proud of her husband. That is the work of the Holy Spirit. You people will travel to far countries, and I will perform miracles through Sam and Dorthula.

They will testify of Sam's sickness and how I brought Sam back to life and blessed him with a beautiful car.

I gave him the wisdom and knowledge to preach me, Jesus of Nazareth.

Prepare for the trip. It will be a big one for both of you, and I will be right there with you, because I am the one sending you.

Sam is a very good listener, and at all times he is expecting to be filled with the Holy Spirit just to preach my word. That is a great blessing upon him and the members of "the Lord's bible studies."

Janet Janet, mother Dorothy's daughter, would be healed if only she believed in me and that I can do all things. The Lord's bible studies the right place for her if she only believes. A miracle will happen. She just has to stop worrying and look unto Jesus.

Deaconess Donna will not solve her problem. She will have to stop worrying and trust me. Sam has been calling her and her husband, but they refuse to come.

Try to fix your home problems. Sam cannot fix it. Your husband is the head of the house, not your children. Do the right thing and the blessings will begin to overflow.

The Lord's bible studies will grow worldwide because of the trip. Sam has a lot of traveling to do. He will preach the word for me. He is good, and I gave him the wisdom and knowledge about the bible.

Sam, do not listen to anyone except me. I am the one who brought you back to life, because you have a good spirit towards people. I am very jealous that someone else did not heal you. That's why you do not get you healing from human beings. I did it all for you to preach my word.

Matthew 28:18-20: and Jesus came and spake unto them, saying, all power is given unto me in heaven and in earth. Go ye, therefore, and teach all nations, baptizing them in the name of the father and of the son, and of the Holy Ghost. Teach them to observe all things whatsoever I have commanded you; and Lord, I am with you always, even unto the end of the world. Amen.

God will follow every time you go to preach my word. I was present yesterday and towards the end. Bless with revelation 22:1-2.

Jesus of Nazareth, the holy one of Israel, the first and the last, the God of Abraham, Isaac and Jacob. God is working miracles through Sam and it will continue in the years to come.

Long life for all the members of the Lord's bible studies. Don't you see, I came at the end to bless everyone?

It is coming to light now. I am leaving now. Sam is a good person. He doesn't play with God and he is very serious about the word.

Revelation 22:19: and if any man shall take away from the words 0f the book of this prophecy, God shall take away his part out of the book of life, and out of the holy city, and from the things which are written in this book.

Bye, bye for now. Jesus of Nazareth.

You are very tired, but I will strengthen you for my work. It is not a small job. Bye, bye again, Sam.

## Monday—February 23, 2015

Psalms 118:8: it is better to trust in the Lord than to put confidence in Austin's. Psalms 20:8: they are brought down and fallen, but we are risen and stand upright. Sam, you are very good in the world. That's why I called you to do my work, because you love God. I really prepared you for this job. You suffered so much for me, because I love you. All your past mistakes have been forgiven. You are now a new creature in Christ Jesus.

Angels are always in your apartment. It is blessed. I am with you always. Do not worry. People are jealous of you, but you suffered for this blessing.

Every eye was watching you while you were suffering, but be happy now because I brought you back. How can you receive the blessings from me without suffering? I did it so you will always remember the days that you were sick. That is how I call people to do my work.

Sam, you are very clever to do my work, and I blessed you with the scriptures, the whole bible. Such a gift is so high because you are chosen by my father, God, to work with me, Jesus. You are very intelligent, but you act like you know nothing under any leader.

Sam, God is on your side to perform miracles. Many nations would invite you to come and preach. Don't worry; I will be there with you in spirit. You cannot do the work you are doing now without the Holy Spirit. The spirit is upon you like a fire.

Joseph suffered because of the woman, but later I blessed him. You, Sam, are going to be blessed like any other persons in the bible. No one can do what you are doing now. It is a great calling from my father, God. The angels are all rejoicing because of you, Sam.

You preach the word like you are there.

St. John 14:10-13: believeth thou not that I am in the father, and the father in me. The words that I speak unto you I speak not of myself, but the father that dwelleth in me. He doeth the work.

I gave you wisdom to believe you will do more things in my name. Do not fear anyone, because I am always with you. No one can harm you. Those pastors will fall. Don't you see some of them are sick? It is because of you. They judged you wrongly instead of praying for you.

Sam is so blessed with the word of God. He loves to preach. That is his nature, to preach without ceasing like Paul of tarsus on the road to Damascus.

Acts 9:4-31: and he fell to the earth, and heard a voice saying unto him, Saul, Saul, why persecutes thou me? And he said, who art thou, Lord? And the Lord said, I am Jesus whom thou persecute. It is hard for thee to kick against the pricks.

Sam, the road of salvation. Romans 3:23:

Revelation 22:5-17: and there shall be no night there; and they need no candle, neither light of the sun, for the Lord giveth them light; and they shall reign for ever and ever.

Sam is a prophet and he did not even know it. I laid it on his sister's heart, Heidi, to text him and let him know.

Just be happy about your calling. I have to leave, but I will be back in time for Holy Communion. The members must believe in what you are doing. It is a really serious matter. There is my blood and my body to share with the world.

Isaiah 53:4-5: you should be ready at communion services every week. I love all the members of the Lord's bible studies.

Bye, bye,

*Jesus of Nazareth*

# Monday—February 23, 2015

## ST. JOHN 8:32: YE SHALL KNOW THE TRUTH AND THE TRUTH SHALL MAKE YOU FREE.

I came to establish the truth on earth, but people love the darkness more than the truth. All those who have received me should be in the truth. Otherwise, no kingdom of heaven for them. You cannot live in the flesh and go to heaven. God is a spirit, and all those who choose to follow him should worship him in spirit and in truth. St. John 4:24.

The living water is the word of God, not common water as at Jacob's well. The water can dry up, but my water is everlasting to everlasting.

Heaven and earth shall pass away, but my word stands forever. In the book of genesis it says, in the beginning God created everything in this world that we are now enjoying, but now there is no respect for the creator. But the time is coming very soon when true believers shall worship him in the spirit, not in the flesh.

Romans 12: 1: I beseech you therefore, brethren, by the mercies of God, that ye present your bodies as a living sacrifice, holy, acceptable unto God, which is your reasonable service.

Romans 3:23: for all have sinned, and come short of the glory of God.

How can you say you love God and not trust him? Someone laid down his life for you. You say you do not believe the bible. A time is coming very soon, and sooner than we expect when my father will show his powers on earth.

The churches are destroying the people. There is fornication and adultery, which is the leading factor in the world today. People are making money by the thousands because of illicit sex acts.

I love Sam very much because of what he stands for. He only preaches the gospel of me, Jesus Christ. My father loves Sam so much that he gave him the wisdom about the bible. He is writing every day because I want people to know that I am in the world performing miracles through Sam.

People are planning something about you, Sam, but they will not succeed. No one can harm you. I revealed to Sam that people are worshipping idols in their closets. These are not stories I reveal to Sam in his writings. Sam's preaching will bring a lot of secrets out. That's why they are all afraid of him. Sister Joanne is wasting her time in the church. She has no faith in the gospel because she has not gotten a good leader to teach the word.

Sam cannot do this work without the anointing upon him. He is always in the spirit. The trip would be the greatest trip in his life. Sam, pray and study more to write my words.

The first writing of this book should be finished by June 2016, and the second book in 2018. You will be travelling a lot in the near future. The devil is busy; therefore you should be ready to pray more than arguing. Sam does not belong to the world. He is a changed man unto God. He is blessed from above. Dorthula, be careful about Sam. He cannot help himself in what he is going through in his life. It is all the spirit controlling him.

The Lord's bible studies would be experienced in many cities and the world. Israel is the beginning of everything. I have to leave now, and the angels of the Lord will take over.

Bye, bye for now,

*Tuesday—February 24, 2015*

## THE LORD JESUS CHRIST.

Psalms 12:1-2: help, Lord, for the Godly man ceases for the faithful and fail from among the children of men. They speak vanity, everyone with his neighbor, with flattering lips and with a double heart do they speak.

1 john 1:9: if we confess our sins, he is faithful and just forgives us our sins, and to cleanse us from all unrighteousness.

Confess to the savior of the world. I have to leave. I see the weather is changing to light.

Good bye, Sam.

Until next time, Jesus of Nazareth.

*Wednesday—February 25, 2015*

## WHAT ARE THEY EXPECTING FROM ME WHEN THEY DIE?

Matthew 7:21-34: not everyone that saith unto me, Lord, Lord, shall enter into the kingdom of heaven, but he that doeth the will of my father, which is in heaven, many will say to me in that day, Lord, Lord, have we not prophesied in thy name? And in thy name have cast out devils? And in thy name done many wonderful works?

You can play with a toy, but not with me, Jesus. I came to do exactly what my father and your father sent me to do for your sake. If you deny me here, I would deny you when you die.

Revelation 22:13-16: I am alpha and omega, the beginning and the end, the first and the last. Blessed are they who do his commandments that they may have a right to the tree of life, and may enter through the gates into the city.

In the Lord's bible studies I gave Sam the knowledge and wisdom to teach the word. Don't you see he is a different person now? I will strengthen him every day to do my work for me.

Joshua 1:8: the book of the law shall not depart out of thy mouth; but thou shall meditate therein day and night that thou mayest observe to do according to all that is written therein; for then thou shall make thy way prosperous, and then thou shalt have good success.

Deuteronomy 28:5-10: blessed shall be thy basket and thy store. Blessed shalt thou be when thou comest in, and blessed shalt thou be when thou goest out.

I am watching everything that is going on in the world today. Remember the days of Noah? The same thing will happen again, because my father is not pleased about the world and the wickedness that is taking over with satanic forces turning the minds of my people.

Christians do not even have time to call upon me. They do not even know how they are living and do not even recognized their existence in the world and their purpose of life. The world is in a very sad situation.

Some preachers are preaching that salvation is free. It is not free. Somebody died for sinners. I, Jesus, died and you people treat me like you have no clue. I will deny you in front of my father in the kingdom.

Preachers are using my name and the gospel to make money every moment.

1 timothy 6:10: for the love of money is the root of all evil; which while some coveted after they have erred from the faith, and pierced themselves through with many sorrows.

The love of money is evil, and this leads to destruction, I say again.

Mark 8:36: for what shall it profit a man if he shall gain the whole world and lose his own soul? It does not make any sense. The whole world is corrupt because Christians do not pray enough. They refuse to pray to me, yet they want quick results. They have to pray to me more with honor, and then I will hear from them.

I came to do everything perfect because my father is good and perfect. He loves the world because he is the one who created it.

St. John 3:16: for God so loved the world that he gave his only begotten son that whosoever believeth in him should not perish, but have everlasting life. Don't you see from the beginning he created heaven and earth? He gave people the lovely creation for them to enjoy, but rather human beings have corrupted the world my father created. They love themselves more than to worship my father who created them.

Heaven is a beautiful place to live, but there are conditions to go there. You can say to me that you are a Christian, but when you die you will know if you were a true Christian. Do not fool yourself; it is not easy to enter into my place of holiness. You ought to be fully holy, and then you will have a mansion awaiting you. Find time to read my word and pray earnestly and believe.

Christians do not have enough faith to believe that I am still alive and working miracles in the world today. I am always here in the world, but you do not have spiritual eyes to see me, because I am a spirit.

Sam, I have shown you a lot of signs. Sometimes you feel what is happening to me. Your long suffering has caused me reward you with a beautiful car for you to enjoy. I taught you to drive again. I took away the nervousness from you the day you started to drive. The car belongs to me, Jesus. Do not allow just anybody to drive it without them having the Holy Spirit.

Upon you the Holy Spirit is different. It is a special calling in your life that I have put upon you. Try to always do good for people who are in need of help and I will greatly reward you.

I brought those girls to you, and one of them would be a prophetess for me, whether she likes it or not. I am the one controlling everybody's lives in this wicked world.

Continue to do the good work I have given you to do. Sam, you are a very good person, but people do not recognize you, that are why I choose you to do my work that I have left behind.

Matthew 28:18-20: and Jesus came and spake unto them saying; all power is given unto me in heaven and in earth; go ye, therefore, and teach all nations, baptizing them in the name of the father, and the son, and the holy ghost. Teaching them to observe all things whatsoever I have commanded you; and lo, I am with you always, even unto the end of the world. Amen.

Your brother-in -law is in great fear of you, Sam. He fears you like a lion in a cage. Imagine he allowed you to preach that Sunday in Middletown Baptist church in august, 2015.

That would be the end of that church. He is going to invite you again. I will prepare you in the spirit to preach hard on them, and abolish fornication in the church from the so called leaders.

You had already prophesied to Raymond that Friday night before her marriage that it would not work. She did not listen to you, and see what happened. The marriage is now on the rocks.

Some ministers are playing with their lives and Sam Ahulu, 'the miracle of Jesus Christ,' because they know they will be exposed, as they and the churches are doing things secretly. I am watching them, but how can they hide from me, Jesus?

2 chronicles 16:9: for the eyes of the Lord run to and fro the whole earth, to shew himself strong on behalf of them whose heart is perfect toward him, herein thou hast done foolishly, therefore from henceforth thou shalt have wars.

I am a spirit travelling all over the world, because the world belongs to me, Jesus. I have full control over the whole world.

The days are getting shorter. You all better wake up and pray to the Almighty God. Every day people wake up and do not have time for me, only for themselves. But judgement day is coming very soon.

Matthew 12:36: but I say unto you that every idle word that men speak, they shall give account thereof in the day of judgement.

Revelation 20:11-13: and I saw a great white throne, and him that sat on it, from whose face the earth and the heaven fled away; and there was found no place for them.

Romans 14:10-12: but why dost thou judge thy brother? Or why dost thou set at naught they brother? For we shall all stand before the judgement seat of Christ. For, as it is written, as I live, sayeth the Lord, every knee shall bow to me, and every tongue shall confess to God. So then every one of us shall give account 0f himself to God.

## Sunday—March 15, 2015

Matthew 28: 1-20: in the end of the Sabbath, as it began to dawn toward the first day of the week, came Mary Magdalene and the other Mary to see the sepulcher, and behold, there was a great earthquake, for the angel of the Lord descended from heaven, and came and rolled back the stone from the door and sat upon it.

On the morning of the resurrection, the two women went to the tomb searching for Jesus and the angels from heaven, asked who they were searching for, and they said Jesus, the angels announced to them that he was not there, but he had risen.

Go and tell his disciples that they should meet him at the place he showed them. The women went down to the disciples and they also came and saw the empty tomb, and they believed that Jesus Christ had risen from the grave. The first in the history of mankind. Later Jesus met two men walking on the road and he asked them, "What are you talking about?" They said to Jesus, "Are you a stranger in Israel that they have crucified? The savior of the world, Jesus of Nazareth?"

It is a miracle for the world to know that I am alive. I am alpha and omega. Revelation 22:13

Sam, you better prepare for the future. My father chose you to preach the word, and the angels in heaven rejoice when you preach Jesus, the author and finisher of our faith. I am watching and looking at everything going on in the world today. People are very disobedient and disrespectful; refusing to accept me as Lord and savior after all I have done for them. In the beginning, the old commandments instructed children to honor their parents that their life would be long upon earth.

I am a witness for that in the kingdom of God. I came to this satanic world to prove that I am still alive in the kingdom, and I am the light of the world.

People do not play with Sam. He is a chosen one to work for me and to spread the good news to the world. You are very clever, especially giving the word. Speaking Jesus is your food. You are very humble. I am proud of you. Dorthula does not understand that God is using you. The only thing Sam thinks about is to preach Jesus. Yes, people should know who is the founder of this organization and also that the whole world belongs to him. He came to prove that there is a heaven and earth. Choose the one you like. No forcing. It should be of your own free will that would lead you to either heaven or hell. St. John 3:16. The love of God is everywhere, which is seen in his creation of the world. God is always directing what one must do to have eternal life. St. Mark 1:15: the time is fulfilled and the kingdom of God is at hand; repent ye; and believe the gospel.

Sam will go to a lot of world conferences of Christian religion in the future. The trip was an open door for you, Sam. The car is one reward. The house is coming in the near future. Sam, do not add anything to your holiness.

Everyone, be careful of Sam's anointing from above (heaven) to preach me.

I will strengthen you, Sam, to do my work. You are qualified to do it. He knows the bible. Sam has devoted his time for the Lord's work.

Holiness is the key to heaven; there is no other way.

Deny yourself, as I also deny myself to come into this world to die for mankind. Revelation 22:1-5: and he showed me a pure river of water of life, clear as crystal, proceeding out of the throne of God and of the lamb. In the midst of the street of it, and on either side of the river, there was the tree of life, which bore twelve manners of fruits, and yielded her fruits every month, and the leaves of the tree were for the healing of the nations.

Jeremiah 23:1-5: woe be unto the pastors that destroy and scatter the sheep of my pasture, sayeth the Lord. Therefore, thus sayeth the Lord God of Israel against the pastors that feed my people; ye have scattered my flock and driven them away, and have not visited them. Behold, I will visit upon you the evil of your doings, sayeth the Lord.

More blessings are coming, Sam. Continue to do the good work. Preach me, Jesus.

Bye, bye,

Jesus of Nazareth.

## Sunday—March 1, 2015

The devil has played tricks on people's minds, and they believe what he says. He is a liar from the beginning, and even now. Some people are not serious about me, Sam, when I talk and tell them things. They are stubborn and are being led in the wrong direction of life because of Satan.

I have to leave now. Sam, be a good boy. I love you. Continue to preach the word. Dorthula is now trying to understand you, because you are always in the spirit.

Bye, bye,

Jesus of Nazareth.

## Monday—March 2, 2015

**BY HIS GRACE. THE WORD.**

Don't you know the words I speak to you? From the beginning it is the word which my father spoke to create everything. I came and dwell among you. Please, Sam, preach the words, and people will hear you.

Matthew 24:35: heaven and earth shall pass away, but my words shall not pass away.

St. John 8:32: and ye shall know the truth, and the truth shall make you free.

People still do not believe what I am saying through you, Sam. Your prophecy was true from the first day you went to the hospital.

Sister Kelly is a double-minded person. She is under the preaching of someone who is not of me. How can she grow spiritually to have a better understanding of me through the word?

Some pastors do not know me spiritually because I have not revealed myself to them. I don't reveal myself to womanizers who preach garbage! That is why they want to kill you, Sam, but they cannot harm you. There is a fire around you which is from above. All the angels are rejoicing when Sam is preaching the word. My father is just very happy about you standing powerfully and reaching me.

Sam loves to proclaim the word. Sam has been killed with the mouth of a lot of people, but because of his anointing no one can harm him. I do not know why Sam can preach me like that. The one thing about him is that he is very humble and speaks less. He only speaks when he wants to. He always wants to know how he stands to preach and change the lives of so many people.

The world is full of evil, frustration and immorality.

Sam has no time for the things of this world. He only wants to live a holy life and to speak and preach in big places.

I was present yesterday on Sunday, march 2, 2015. See how he demonstrates Moses and the Ten Commandments when he came from Mount Sinai? It seems like Sam was there. That is what we call faith. Sam puts all his life in the word. The light upon him is very heavy all the time. He always wants to talk about me, Jesus.

## Monday—March 2, 2015

It is a blessing for someone like Sam to preach like Apostle Paul. People will come from all over the world to see and hear him preach. I have given him the wisdom and knowledge after a long sickness. Spiritual sickness is worse than anything one can compare any other with.

St. John 11:4: when Jesus heard that, he said that sickness is no it unto death, but for the glory of God, that the son of God might be glorified thereby.

Sam will be able to stand so he can do much more for me in the near future. He just loves to preach the word.

Romans 8:32: he that spared not his own son, but delivered him up for us all, how shall he not also freely gives us all things?

Galatians 3:21-25: is the law then against the promises 0f God? God forbid. For if there had been a law given which could have given life, verily righteousness should have been by the law.

Revelation 20:1-15: and I saw an angel come down from heaven, having the key of the bottomless pit and great chain in his hand.

The ministry. If Sam was funny I would never call him to represent me in Israel. Don't you know the whole world will be coming to this occasion at the world conference center? That is where miracles will happen through me in Sam. You, Dorthula, will have to give a testimony to let people know of Sam's suffering, and for people to know that I am alive in the world today observing all things.

This trip will not be a romantic journey; it will be a journey for you to learn about me and my life, and how I suffered in this world.

I, Jesus, have revealed myself to Dorthula several times for you to believe the work I am doing through Sam.

How can the preachers collect 20% of tithes form their members? They are cheating the members to make money for themselves. Sam is always speaking the truth of the gospel about the so-called ministers without the Holy Spirit.

Sam has no time for these foolish-minded preachers. Sam is better than them. Sam likes to preach and that is what he is doing. I called him, and my father gave him the scriptures all in his head to memorize for his preaching and teaching.

St. John 14:26: but the comforter, which is the holy ghost, whom the father will send in my name, he shall teach you all things and bring all things to your remembrance. Whatsoever I have said unto you.

No other minister can do that. Sam is very clever. He studies a lot about me. He does not play with the word.

St. John 6:63: it is the spirit that quickeneth, and the flesh profiteth nothing. The words that I speak unto you, they are spirit, and they are life.

Matthew 28: 1-20: in the end of the Sabbath, as it began to dawn toward the first day of the week, came Mary Magdalene and the other Mary to see the sepulcher and, behold there was a great earthquake; for the angel of the Lord descended from heaven and came and rolled back the stone from the door, and sat upon it.

Those three women, who came to the tomb, let it be an example for the world to see, that when someone does good unto you, you have to appreciate it. The three women came to the tomb because they knew what Jesus Christ had done for them. Of the ten lepers that were cleansed, only one came back, to thank me, Jesus. Everyone needs a thank you.

Merriam suffered because she spoke against the servant of God.

Numbers 12: 1-10: and Merriam and Aaron spake against Moses because 0 f the Ethiopian woman whom he had married.

Aaron, brother of Moses, was a coward to organize such a group to go against the Ten Commandments. Moses did his job, but he did not reach the promised land. It is better to listen keenly to God when he speaks.

No more arguments, Dorthula, or else. Understand Sam. He is always in the spirit; that is what we call blessing from God.

Time is running out. It is time for people to stop fighting and study the word.

*Monday—March 2, 2015*

**ONE MORE TIME.**

St. John 6:63: it is the spirit that quickeneth, the flesh profiteth nothing. The words that I speak unto you, they are spirit and they are life.

Jeremiah 23:1-5: woe be unto the pastors that destroy and scatter the sheep of my pasture, sayeth the Lord.

I am leaving now, Sam, bye, bye,

The faithful servant of Jesus Christ.

## Tuesday—March 3, 2015

Matthew 11:28: come unto me, all ye that labor and are heavy laden, and I will give you rest.

Sam, what you told Sean is the truth. He needs to pray more. This boy loves me so much like a father. I, Jesus, am going to bless him. Within one year I will give him a promotion in his job. The thing about him is that he rushes to do things too much. He has to take things one day at a time.

Sam has suffered so much, and that is why I am blessing him so much now. The purpose of the trip to the holy land is to prepare you, Sam, to preach me, Jesus, to the world. You are so humble, Sam, but you never like to be noticed or recognized when you are doing my work. You will preach without opening the bible, because I have given you the wisdom and the knowledge, and to bring everything to your memory. You love to preach me anywhere you go.

The so-called ministers that are against you will die because they judged you wrongfully. I love you, Sam. You always do everything I tell you to do.

Do you remember what happened in the Garden of Eden? My father warned them not to touch the forbidden tree. The devil came and deceived eve, and he twisted the words of God. She yielded to the devil, and that is why the world is suffering today. It is total disobedience in the sight of God.

My son went to the cross for all mankind, but it seems no one cares about his suffering. St. John 1:29: behold the Lamb of God, which taketh away the sins of the world.

When Christ was suffering, no one would like to suffer like he did. Sam is healed by the stripes of our Lord and savior Jesus Christ.

Sam is the one I have chosen to lead this organization, the Lord's bible studies.

The whole world is coming to an end soon. Everyone should be prepared. Do not call Sam a liar. It is prophecy. It can be years from now, but it will happen. My father loves Sam so much because of his faith in God. He loves to preach and I accept him for that.

The first book should be published in December 2015. The second book in June 2016. I will strengthen you, Sam, to do my work.

Good bye, and good night, Jesus of Nazareth.

## Good Friday—April 3, 2015

**THIS IS GOOD FRIDAY FOR SAM.**

St. John 14:6: Jesus sayeth, I am the way, the truth, and the life; no man cometh unto the father, but by me.

Matthew 26:35: peter said unto him, though I should die with thee, I will not deny thee. Likewise, also all the disciples.

Matthew 24:35-42: heaven and earth shall pass away, but my word shall not pass away.

In the bathroom that morning at 6:35 a.m., I was crying bitterly when I remembered how he, Jesus, suffered for us, and we do not regard him as somebody who did so much for us. The Day of Judgment will not be nice. Some people think it is a joke. I came that they must escape it, but still they do not want to listen to me. My simple message is just repentance. Mark 1:15: turn from your ways of living and come to me. You refuse me, so how can you enter into heaven if you do not know the principles of God? Obedience is better than sacrifice.

Matthew 7:21: not every one that sayeth unto me, Lord, Lord, shall enter into the kingdom of heaven, but he that doeth the will of my father which is in heaven.

I continue to say, I am the way to the kingdom of God. The world is on the verge of collapsing, but people do not see it, because they are in the darkness. When you enter into a dark room, what do you do? You put on the light. I am the light of the world, but people refuse to accept it. The creation alone, you can see the loving God who created the whole world and yet people do not rim. Noah's an 'fs coming back again. People will be shocked, when the true children of God will enter the ark not built by human beings, but by God himself. Do not ask me how it is going to happen? God can do anything he wants to do. He is supernatural. He is the God of Abraham, Isaac and Jacob. The same God of thousand generations. You can never understand the wonders of God.

Isaias 55:8: for my thoughts are not your thoughts, neither are your ways my ways, sayeth the Lord. Just accept it and believe.

I am using Sam to write all these for a book, "God's wonderful world". The boy, Sam, suffered so many years, but one thing. He believes in me so much, and that's why I brought him back to do my work and stand for me, to preach very hard sermons.

To the congregation, the ministers and the people, Sam, be very careful of the churches you go to, because on those days you go there will be a lesson for everyone.

I love Sam and Dorthula working together to do my work. The duty is to be as a supreme being to guide people in how to live holy for me, Jesus, to gain eternal life. The key to heaven is me and no one else. Read again and again. St. John 14:6. The living water St. John 4:10: the woman at Jacob's well.

The Sea of Galilee and the Garden of Eden is still functioning, but no one can see it. It is all spiritual in the middle of the great continent of Africa. Sam, do the work I have given you to do. No one can harm you. I am always with you day and night.

Those ministers who are planning against you will suffer a terrible death. How can you destroy someone who has a special gift from heaven? I gave it to Sam because he loves the "word" (bible). He always wants to learn more about me. This boy is a blessing to the whole world. Sam is a good man, only his "temper," especially if you are playing with God. He would even like to kill you.

The love of God is in my servant. He is doing the will of the one who called him. God is good.

Bye, bye,

Sam.

# PRAISING THE LORD— STANDING ON THE EDGE

Joshua 3:7-17: and the Lord said unto Joshua, this day will I begin to magnify thee in the sight of all Israel. When the children of Israel were standing on the edge of river Jordan and wanted to cross over to Canaan, the promised land, they were standing behind the edge not knowing what to do.

Joshua 3:17: and the priests that bore the ark of the covenant of the Lord stood firm on dry ground in the midst of Jordan. The New Year message to you, by his race you will cross over the obstacles in your path, a day God has ordained before you were born into this world.

Matthew 17:20: because of your unbelief, for verily I say unto you, if ye have the faith as a grain of mustard seed, ye shall say unto this mountain, remove hence to yonder place, and it shall remove, and nothing shall be impossible unto you.

Sam, all your enemies are afraid of you because I have brought you back to life. They fear the gospel you preach, which I gave to you as a special gift from heaven. No one can recite the scriptures like you. You are a very good person.

I call you in the morning to pray, and you are very surprised by what is happening in your life. You have no control over it.

It is a very hard job to win souls, but you are in the spirit. Therefore, you can do it. The world is corrupt and dangerous. Be careful. People are talking about you. They were all expecting you to die. They'd rather go before you. You have a lot of jobs to do for me, like apostle Paul did for me. Do not worry, I am always with you.

No temptations will come to you. I will destroy it. Everybody loves

You, because the light is upon you.

You will perform wonders in the years to come. People will come to you for prayers. Do it by faith in me, Jesus. I will never fail you. You have suffered so long. The car is a reward for you and Dorthula.

Sam, prepare to work in the summer. I will bring in the souls for you to teach them the word of God. I will give you wisdom to do that. I used john to encourage you that you will not die. I like that courage in you, Sam. You have to talk about my suffering. I am always present at Holy Communion. Nobody sees me, but I am always there. Those who refuse to come, leave them alone. They are losing before they realize it will be too late.

Bye, bye,

Sam

*Wednesday—March 4, 2015*

**WHERE ARE YOU RUNNING TO?**

Psalms 139:7-10: whether shall I go from thy spirit? Or whether shall I flee from thy presence? If I ascend up into the heaven, thou art there. If I make my bed in hell, behold, thou art there. If I take the wings of the morning and dwell in the uttermost parts of the sea; even there shall thy hand lead me, and thy right hand shall hold me.

A lot of people are running from me, but where are they going? I am everywhere at all times. It is better to confess your sins than to run from me.

St. Mark 1:15: the time is fulfilled, and the kingdom of God is at hand; repent ye, and believe the gospel. I came to ask people to repent and come to me. Rather, they choose the devil instead of me, Jesus, the giver of life. Each and every one is going to face me at the judgment seat of Christ. Many know in their hearts that God is merciful, therefore I will forgive them. If not, then why salvation would be preached to people. It is my spirit that moves in every direction upon the earth. Remember the woman at Jacob's well?

St. John 4:7-10: there cometh a woman of Samaria to draw water; Jesus sayeth unto her, "give me to drink."

The living water is the water of life.

Sam is the e greatest of the apostles to preach the word and the truth. He is a faithful servant of the Lord. Everybody in the kingdom is happy because of Sam.

God servant.

John preached about the remission of sins, but I came to baptize in the name of the father, the son and the Holy Spirit. Yet people are not seeing the goodness of God. If you allow yourself, God will use you to do his work on earth. He has the power to do what he wants to do.

The only way for someone to enter the kingdom is to repent and be baptized.

St. John 3:5-8: Jesus answered, verily, verily, I say unto thee, except a man be born of water and the spirit, he cannot enter into the kingdom of God. The spirit of God is moving upon the face of the earth, and people should realize that God is nearer than they are expecting. My spirit travels everywhere at all times. You must be born of the spirit. The flesh profiteth nothing.

Sam, do not be afraid. Don't you see the light shines brightly for you to see to write every word from me? We are here, us angels sent by God to declare this message to you, Sam.

Dorthula should testify about your long sickness from the year 2003-2014 when the Lord spoke to me one afternoon, September 15, 2014.

The reward of your sickness is the car that I have given to you and Dorthula. Sam is the good shepherd of the people in the Lord's bible studies. Many people would be saved for the kingdom because of Sam's preaching and teachings. Those who are against him will suffer at my hands. I work in Sam so people will see more reality in the work Sam is doing.

Sam is a very happy man because of what I have done for him. He really suffered for this blessing. Sam is a good person. The trip to Israel would be beneficial for him and the Lord's bible studies. John is the one who the Holy Spirit worked through to encourage Sam that he was not going to die. John is a spiritual son to Sam. This boy loves him so much. John regarded Sam as a prophet a long time ago, even when Sam was very sick. He always have the hope that one day God will bring you back to preach more than before.

Debra loves Sam very much, because she sees that Uncle Sam is a good person and he is always praying for her. She is very proud of Uncle Sam and my aunt Dottie.

Sam, try to do everything right in the Lord, because your calling is a very special calling from me, Jesus.

Every born-again believer should keep his or her body holy, because your body is the temple of God.

Bye, bye,

Sam

Going back home to be with my father. God demonstrates his love to us.

St. John 3:16: for God so loved the world that he gave his only begotten son, that whosoever believeth in him should not perish, but have everlasting life.

Love is the root of everything. Look for yourself and see the love God has for you. Look at the animals and see the love God has for them. When you look at your children you see the love of God. God demonstrates his love towards mankind. He sends his only begotten son, Jesus Christ, to die for us. He was our substitute on the cross to pass us from death to life. The love he had for Lazarus, he raised him to life. Because of love, he did not open his mouth. Love stretches long and there is no end.

Now, I am right here at present in the spirit. Have the Holy Communion now. The angels are watching. Do it quickly.

## *Friday—March 6, 2015*

**FOR GOD SO LOVED THE WORLD**

St. John 3:16: for God so loved the world that he gave his only begotten son, that whosoever believeth in him should not perish, but have everlasting life.

God gave his son to sacrifice his own life for us sinners. He freely released the ghost to his father in his final days on the earth. The love of God surpasses everything. He came to his own to give life for those who believe in him.

Isaiah 53:4-5: surely he hath borne our grieves and carried our sorrows; yet we did esteem him stricken, smitten of God and afflicted, but he was wounded for our transgressions. He was bruised for our inequities; the chastisement 0f our peace was upon him, and with his stripes we are healed.

Isaiah 9:6: the price of our peace was upon him. Jesus did a lot in dying for our sins. He was slain like a lamb to the slaughter, and as a sheep before his shearers. He was condemned to the to death on the cross to save dying souls. His blood washed away our sins and purified our bodies by faith.

He came to the world because of love. He offered his life as a sacrifice to those who accept him as their personal savior. The very hour you accept him, you become a new creature in him.

The world is sinking in sin gradually every day. The final day is coming. Come follow me. Love is the greatest thing on earth. Love has no enemies, love does not cheat, love has no boundaries, and love is pure and perfect.

The devil can use anyone to destroy you, Sam. The anointing is very powerful on you. You are always in the spirit. God is everywhere. Isaiah 43:2.

Good night and good bye,

Sam

## Friday—March 6, 2015

**IN THE BEGINNING**

St. John 1:1: in the beginning was the word, and the word was with God, and the word was God.

The word is God, and God is life; he came into existence to create life in the form of human beings. He giveth his own life for us, but we refuse to accept life in the one who died for us.

He, Jesus, came into this world and was born in a manger. No place of his owns did he have to lay his head. He had to share a place with the animals for his birth without modern gears.

This was prophesied 700 years before he came. He came unto his own, but they refused him. Therefore, he turned to the gentiles. He grew with wisdom and knowledge. At the age of 12 he started his ministry in the synagogue in Israel. He was there with his parents for the passover, but after three days his parents discovered the he, Jesus, was not among the crowd, so they returned to Jerusalem seeking him and they saw him in the temple in the midst of the doctors, both hearing and asking questions. The parents asked him why he had done that. He answered, "Wouldn't you allow me to do my father's business?" The parents then discovered that he was not just a child, but one that was sent from heaven to do miracles. His earthly father was a carpenter, and he had learned the trade from his father.

After the death of john, he started his ministry preaching repentance of sins.

St. Mark 1:15: and saying, the time is fulfilled, and the kingdom of God is at hand; repent ye, and believe the gospel.

Many have heard the call of repentance, but the devil has blinded their minds not to accept him as Lord and savior.

He continued his mission when he chose his first disciples. Simon called peter and his brother and Andrew, and he continued on to choose more disciples. He was the messiah, the forthcoming king, bringing truth to the world.

Acts 1:2: until the day in which he was taken up; after that he, through the Holy Ghost, have given commandments unto the apostles whom he had chosen.

The promise of the Holy Spirit.

Acts 1:8: but ye shall receive power. After that the Holy Ghost is come upon you, and ye shall be witnesses unto me, both in Jerusalem and in allju9aea, and in Samaria, and unto the uttermost parts of the earth.

Acts 2:4: and they were all filled with the Holy Ghost and began to speak with other tongues as the spirit gave them utterance.

Matthew 28:18: and Jesus came and spake unto them, saying, all power is given unto me in heaven and in earth.

Sam continues to do my work. The blessings are coming. Bye, bye Jesus of Nazareth.

## Saturday—March 7, 2015

Genesis 2:16-17: and the Lord God commanded the man, saying, of every tree of the garden, thou mayest freely eat, but of the tree of the knowledge of good and evil, thou shalt not eat of it, for in the day that thou eatest thereof, thou shalt surely die.

I, God, brought a woman to Adam not to be lonely, but for a help meet. Eve was misled by the devil, which twisted the word of God, and they both ate from the forbidden tree, which I already warned them not to touch or even to look at it.

From generation to generation the tree of life is the keeper of the world. It is still in central Africa today.

I am the beginning and the last.

Did you see how the Holy Ghost work come in to work with Sam, and then to the three women at the tomb? Many people will think that since God is a merciful God, then why did he send Adam and eve out of the garden? Do not forget that he had already warned them against what they should not do. The Lord then sent him forth from the Garden of Eden to till the ground from whence he was taken. Did you expect God to beg them to stay in the garden? He had already forewarned them. He is God almighty, and he will do whatever he wants to do.

When he created the world in six days, he saw it and said it is good. God is good and his love lasts forever and forever. He is the everlasting God of Abraham, Isaac and Jacob, the alpha and the omega. God is a good father who truly loves his creation after what our first parents did in disobeying him. He drove out the mand replaced at the east gate of the Garden of Eden, cherubim's and a flaming sword, which turned every way to keep the way of the tree of life.

Adam was 930 years old when he died, and eve was over 700 years old. What we inherited from our first parents was sin, but through the son, the Lord Jesus Christ, brings us back home to the father. Jesus came in a simple manner as a little boy, but he is God himself, and he came to dwell among us for thirty-three and a half years.

After his resurrection he said, "Peace unto you." In the book of john 10:10-21. St. John 15:1-10: Jesus remembers the fig tree when it bore no fruit, and he cursed it down. The same applies to anyone who does not bear fruit. You will be cut down; therefore I say unto you, bear fruits.

Jesus started his first ministry with a great word, "repentance." Mark 1:15: turn away from the way you are going and follow me.

Revelation 3:20: behold, I stand at the door and knock. If any man hear my voice and open the door, I will come in to him and sup with him, and he with me. John preached the remissions of sins, but I came to preach about the Holy Spirit.

Closing the door to me is fine, but a day is coming when heaven's door will be closed and that will be the end of the devil. He will be locked away for a thousand years and the children of Christ will be resurrected. No more crying, no more sickness, but life eternal.

The work you are doing, Sam, is a very hard work, but continues to do it. A big reward is coming your way. The gateway to the world has been opened. Enter into it, Sam, and preach without ceasing. I will give you strength to preach my word.

Heaven and earth shall pass away, but my word shall not pass away.

Good bye, Sam

Sunday holy communion. Preach the word to change the lives of people. It is going to be.

*Saturday—March 7, 2015*

**THE RIVERS OF NO RETURN**

Exodus 1:1: now, these are the names of the children of Israel, which came into Egypt. Every man and his household came with Jacob.

The God of Abraham, Isaac and Jacob is also the God and father of our Lord and savior Jesus Christ, and they which are of the same faith, the same are the children of Abraham. He loves them from the beginning of time to the end of time.

Matthew 28:18-20: and Jesus came and spake unto them, saying, "All power is given unto me in heaven and in earth."

The children of Israel were under the bondage of the Egyptian king pharaoh for 450 years. The Lord prepared a leader, Moses, to deliver them from the hands of the Egyptians. The Lord heard their cries and sent deliverance for them.

Moses ran from Egypt after killing an Egyptian, and went and hid in the wilderness.

Moses spent 40 years in the wilderness before I revealed myself to him to deliver my chosen people from slavery to the promised land. This was a very important job for Moses. It took a long time to prepare him for this task.

The children of Israel were stiff-necked and stubborn. They worshipped the Gods of the Amorites, and were marrying their daughters. When I asked then now to do so in that region, I then revealed myself to Moses on Mount Sinai.

In the time of joseph, each of his brothers died, ending that generation, but their descendants had multiplied gradually.

The new king of Egypt knew nothing about joseph or what he had done. The king told his people that the Israelites were becoming a threat to Egypt. The Egyptians made the Israelites their slaves hoping to put them down under heavy burdens. They served the Israelites in building the cities. Pharaoh, the king of Egypt, gave orders to the midwives that when they helped the Hebrew women that they should kill all the baby boys as soon as they were born and save only the girls. Because the midwives feared God, they refused to obey the king, so they allowed the boys to live, too. A beautiful baby boy was born and was hidden for three months in a basket along the edge of the river Nile.

St. John 1:18: no man hath seen God at any time; the only begotten son, who is in the bosom of the father, he hath declared him.

Moses went to convey the message to the people from God that he would take the Israelites into a close and peculiar relationship with God.

Moses came and called for the elders of Israel, and the Lord told him that he would come in a thick cloud. This is the inauguration Of the art of the ancient church. He is the great and terrible God. In the third day, in the morning, there was thunder and lightning.

Matthew 17:5: while he yet spake, behold, a bright cloud overshadowed them, and behold a voice out of the cloud, which said, this is my beloved son in whom I am well pleased. Hear ye him with the voice of the trumpet. Moses brought the people out of the camp to meet with God.

Exodus 20:1-2: and God spake all these words, saying, I am the Lord thy God, which have brought thee out of the land of Egypt, out of the house of bondage.

Exodus 30:30: and thou shalt anoint Aaron and his sons, and consecrate them that they may minister unto me in the priest's office.

## Wednesday—February 25, 2015

More earthquakes will be coming soon to destroy those who do not believe the gospel. Don't you know that someone created the world?

Genesis 1:20-28: and God said, let the waters bring forth abundantly, the moving creature that hath life, and fowl that fly above the earth in the open firmament of heaven.

My father should have strike, but Jesus is at all times making intercessions for the world, because I shed my own blood to save all mankind. Why don't you people believe in God with all your hearts and enjoy the beautiful creation, the sea, the mountains, the trees and the animals? At least someone should have recognized what I did thousands of years ago, and still people do not respect and know that I am in charge of the whole universe. Christians should pray more. There is too much fooling around, no time for God, but my father has time for the human beings whom he created.

Acts 9:1-20: and Saul, yet breathing out threats and slaughter against the disciples of the Lord, went unto the high priest.

You see, when Saul was working for the leaders of the Jews, he persecuted Jesus on the way to Damascus. I called him on the crossroad to Damascus with a voice from heaven, but those around him did not hear the voice, because I called him to be my chosen vessel, to continue the work I left behind to preach both to the Jews and the gentiles on his missionary journey to various villages and cities, and to proclaim that Jesus Christ is the messiah, the savior of the world.

St. John 1:29-30: the next day john saw Jesus coming unto him, and sayeth, behold the Lamb of God, which taketh away the sin of the world. This is whom I said, after me cometh a man which is preferred before me; for he was before me.

The same thing applies to you, Sam. I allowed the devil to put that sickness on you for many years so you would have the fear of me, Jesus. I chose you a long time ago to work for me, because your word is your bond. Those are the people I want to do my work for me. Many Christians asked why I chose peter to be a leader, and he was the one who was going to betray me. Yes, everyone has faults in their lives, but he was very clever to win souls. That is the reason why I came into this world so people might have a choice to enter into the kingdom of heaven according to their beliefs. St. John 3:16: I am the way, the truth, and the life; no man cometh unto the father, but by me.

If you love me, keep my commandments.

I want holy people to do my work. Don't you know your body is the temple of God? Why don't you keep it holy? I do not dwell in an unclean vessel. I came to this world, because I love this world my father created, but people have turned themselves against me, especially the ministers. They are the worst people. They are doing their own thing to attract people to get money, collecting 20% instead of 10% according to the law of God. They hesitate to go to the highways to win souls for the Lord. They sit in high places and wear expensive robes to show themselves up. Their reward is right here in the world, not in the kingdom.

Revelation 22:12: and behold, I come quickly; and my reward is with me, to give every man according as his works shall be.

# MOSES AND THE BURNING BUSH

One day Moses was tending to the flocks of his father-in-law, metro, the priest of the midianites, and he went deep into the wilderness near Sinai, the mountain of God; and the angel of the Lord appeared to him in a flame of fire out of the midst of a bush. Moses was amazed because the bush was engulfed in flames, but it did not burn. Moses then said to himself, "why isn't the bush burning? I must go and see." When the Lord saw that Moses turned aside to see, God called to him out of the midst of the bush and said, "Moses, Moses," and he answered, "Here am I."

He said, "Do not come closer. Take your sandals off thy feet, for the place whereon thou standest is holy ground." Then Jesus said to him, "I am the God of your ancestors, the God of Abraham, the God of Isaac and the God Jacob." When Moses heard this he hid his face, because he was afraid to look upon God. Then the Lord told Moses, "I have seen the misery of my people in Egypt. I have heard the cry for deliverance from their masters. I am aware of their suffering and I will rescue them from the hands of the Egyptians and their masters out of Egypt. I will send you to pharaoh that you may bring my people out of Egypt."

# MOSES QUESTIONED GOD HOW HE WOULD DO THIS

Isaiah 43:2-3: when thou passeth through the waters, I will be with thee; and through the rivers, they shall not overflow thee; when thou walkest through the fire, thou shalt not be burned, neither shall the flame kindle upon thee. For I am the Lord thy God, the holy one of Israel, the savior.

It is the duty of every Christians in like manner to seek divine directions in all his ways. Exodus 19:1-5: then the Lord said unto Moses, go in unto pharaoh, and tell him, thus sayeth the Lord God of the Hebrews, let my people go, that they may serve me.

# THE ARRIVAL AT MOUNT SINAI

Exodus 19:1-5: in the third month, when the children of Israel were gone forth out of the land of Egypt, the same day came and they went into the wilderness of Sinai. The first passover to proclamation of the law, which leads to Pentecost, which is the new testament church.

St. John 1:17: for the law was given by Moses, but grace and truth came by Jesus Christ.

Acts 2:1: and when the day of Pentecost was fully come, they were all with one accord in one place.

Pharaoh's daughter went to the river to bathe and there she saw the basket floating on the river. She heard the cry of the baby and it touched her heart. She then took the baby to the palace, where it was cared for. God worked it out that Moses' mother is the one who took care of the baby.

They named the baby Moses, meaning he was drawn from water. Matthew 5:7: blessed are the merciful for they shall obtain mercy.

Matthew 11:28: come unto me, all ye that labor and are heavy laden, and I will give you rest.

Good bye, Sam, Jesus of Nazareth.

# JESUS CHRIST CAME TO TAKE THE SINS OF THE WORLD

Paul and john were going to the temple when they saw a man in front of the synagogue asking for money, and Paul said, "silver and gold, have I none, but in the name of Jesus of Nazareth get up and walk." The man got up and started praising God.

Many miracles happened during that period of time. He travelled all over preaching the word of God in all regions of Macedonia, Italy and more places. This was a missionary journey for Paul. He talked with the Greeks about their behavior of the early churches and elsewhere. While travelling over different places Paul said an angel of the Lord spoke to him that no one would die because of the tempest on the seas. Everyone was afraid, but Paul said that the boat would not survive the wind. They all arrived on the shore safely. Apostle Paul suffered at the hands of the authorities, and at one time they stoned him.

This is just like Sam. He suffered for his blessings. Now the anointing is very powerful upon him. He cannot do anything about it, but just to obey and do as I tell him what to do.

Amen. Good bye, Sam.

## Tuesday—March 11, 2015

St. John 11:25-26: Jesus said unto her, I am the resurrection, and the life; he that believeth in me, though he was dead, yet shall he lives.

When the three women went to the tomb early in the morning on Sunday, what did they see? They saw an empty tomb, and the angel asked them, "Who are you looking for, Jesus? He is risen from the dead as he said. Go and tell the disciples to meet me at the place he told them before he died." The disciples rushed to the tomb to see for themselves. They witnessed the empty tomb where Jesus was laid.

Jesus was walking down and he saw two men walking on the road one evening and asked them what was happening, and they said unto him, "Are you a stranger in this town? They said Jesus Christ, the savior of the world, was crucified on Friday evening, believing he is the savior to save the nation of Israel."

He appeared to the disciples when they were locked in a room for fear of the elders. He also appeared to 500 people at once.

He was then taken up to heaven, and siding at the right hand of God, the father. He also asked the disciples not to leave Jerusalem until the Holy Spirit came upon them, because the work they were going to do, they could not do it without the Holy Spirit from heaven. This is the power from heaven.

Acts 2:1-5: and when the day of Pentecost was fully come, they were all with one accord in one place. And suddenly there came a sound from heaven of a rushing mighty wind, and it filled all the houses where they were siding, and there appeared unto them cloven tongues like as of fire, and it sat upon each of them and they were all filled with the holy ghost, and began to speak with other tongues, as the spirit gave them utterance.

The power from above came down, as Jesus promised them, and they stood and preached the good news of Jesus Christ. Peter won 2,000 souls at one time, and they continued on the road to Damascus.

A voice called out from heaven saying to Paul, Paul, why dost thou persecute Jesus?" At that moment he became blind. The people around him heard the voice, but could not see the one speaking. And the spirit of the Lord Paul to the streets called straight to the man of God, Ananias. He prayed for him and his eyes opened. And straight-a-way he stood to preach Jesus as the resurrected one, the son of the living God. The one who died for our sins on the cross. He offered himself to be crucified to save mankind from destroying themselves.

## Thursday—March 12, 2015

Hebrews 11:19: it is impossible to please God without faith. Healing from above.

Isaiah 53:4-5: surely he hath borne our grieves and carried our sorrows; yet we did esteem him stricken, smitten of God and afflicted, but he was wounded for our transgressions. He was bruised for our inequities. The chastisement of our peace was upon him; and with his stripes we are healed.

Jeresophiah 30:17: for I will restore health unto thee; and I will heal thee of thy wounds, sayeth the Lord, because they called thee an outcast, saying this is Zion, whom no man seventh after.

Isaiah 59:1-2: behold, the Lord's hand is not shortened that it cannot save, neither his ear heavy, that it cannot hear, but your inequities have separated between you and your God, and your sins have hidden his face from you, that he will not hear.

Jesus came into this satanic world to do wonders. He healed the sick, he raised the dead. St. John 11:130.

Yes, a miracle at Canaan, at the wedding when Jesus turned the water into wine, yet people doubted him as the son of the living God. He walked on the Sea of Galilee, his birth, which was also a miracle; still people refused to believe all these miracles. People only knew him as a carpenter's son.

The world is full of people who are spiritually sick. They do not believe in my name and that they can have healing. I am a spirit, and can be everywhere at the same time. I am in the world, but no one knows that I am already here. I am just waiting for my father to give me the go ahead to do my work here.

How can I heal you if you do not believe in me? The woman with the issue Of blood was sick for twelve years; she was healed because of her faith in me, that I am the son of the living God.

God said to Moses, I am a consuming fire; therefore I am a living God. The man at the pool was healed because he also believed.

People will be healed if they exercise their faith in me, Jesus.

When I was in the world I prayed every day because the devil is busy, seeking whom he may devour, for he come only to steal, kill and to destroy. St. John 10:10.

He came to me, he will come to you, too, with force, but we have a weapon, which is the word of God, to defeat him.

See what happened in the Garden of Eden? The serpent, which is the devil came to eve and deceived her, which led to spiritual death between them and God. The minute they partook of the fruit of the tree, their eyes were opened. Believe the word of God, for they are life.

From the beginning was the word, and the word was God. He came into the world and dwelt among us. He was on a mission to finish the father's work. He accomplished everything that he set out to do. In the end he said it was finished.

Glory be to the father. I am still in the world healing people, if only they believe in me.

St. John 14:6: Jesus sayeth unto him, I am the way, the truth and the life; no man cometh unto the father, but by me.

I promised the disciples the Holy Ghost to help them finish the work I left behind, and I did it at the right time.

God is merciful. Sam, do not take chances. I have to go. The light is coming.

Bye, bye, Jesus Christ

Psalms 90:1-3: Lord, thou hast been our dwelling place, in all generations.

Last one before prayer at 6:05:

The last commandment I gave to you. Love your neighbor as yourself.

## Sunday—March 15, 2015

The bible says, and everywhere he went he was doing good. He was performing miracles everywhere, like the wedding at Canaan when turned water into wine.

Raising the little girl from death, the wind obeyed him when he and the disciples were at sea. The disciples said, what manner of man is this that even the winds and the sea obeyed him? Matthew 8:27.

He, Jesus, faced palate with love for mankind, yet he opened not his mouth.

St. John 3:16: for God so loved the world that he gave his only begotten son, that whosoever believeth in him should not perish, but have everlasting life. For God sent not his son into the world to condemn the world, but that the world through him might be saved. God is love. Therefore, we must love one another. Thou shall love the Lord thy God with all thy mind, soul and body.

We are told about repentance in the bible. How many people take it serious? Some think it is a joke. I offered up myself to die, and this is not a joke or fairytale.

What is the meaning of repentance? It is the turning away from the direction you are now going, and come follow me, Jesus. Many people do not want to turn from their wicked ways, the ways of the world, to follow me. They love the way they are going, and this is leading them to death, spiritual separation from God. But in the end they will know that it is too late. There will be no repentance in the grave.

Wake up, Sam. They are after you to kill you. They know you are going to be famous, but do not worry, I am with you.

Good bye, Sam, Jesus of Nazareth

## Monday—March 16, 2015

In the beginning God created heaven and the earth, and because 0f love, he created Adam and eve, to be a help mate. Rather, she brought sin into the world by listening to the devil in the form of a serpent. Our suffering today is the cause of a woman, and still they are causing a lot of damage in the world today.

Adam gave excuses to God. The w an you gave to me. I, God did not give you the woman for you to listen to, but she should be a help mate to you. In today's world we are living in, there is only excuse in everything with no time to serve God and to turn unto the maker and the giver of life. People find so many excuses, like my work does not permit me, I have to work, my child is ill, and my business does not allow me time off and all excuses not to worship.

But not all people work on Sundays. People refuse to accept Jesus Christ as their personal savior, because being a Christian one would have to be subjected to the holy God and follow his commandments and live holy. He would be in control of their lives.

They do not have any repentance in their hearts; there are ways to live in the flesh instead of the spirit.

St. John 6:63-65: it is the spirit that quickeneth; the flesh profiteth nothing. The words that I speak unto you, they are spirit and they are life.

Isaiah 1:18-19: come now, let us reason together, sayeth the Lord; though your sins be as scarlet, they shall be as white as snow, though they be red like crimson, they shall be as wool. If ye be willing and obedient, ye shall eat the good of the land.

God is calling us to come together to reason, but the devil has bound them so much that they do not want to come.

Romans 1:22: professing themselves to be wise, they became fools.

Human beings are being controlled by the devil, because we open our hearts to him. In the book of revelation 3:20: behold, I stand at the door and knock. If any man hears my voice and opens the door, I will come in to him, and will rise up with him, and he with me.

Jesus is knocking, but we refuse to open our hearts for him to enter. He cannot force you; you have a choice to make. You have a free will from the beginning in the garden. Your free will can either lead you to heaven or hell.

Matthew 7:21-34: not everyone that sayeth unto me, Lord, Lord, shall enter into the kingdom of heaven, but he that doeth the will of the father, which is in heaven will enter.

Jeresophiah 23:1: woe, be unto the pastors that destroy and scatter the sheep of me of my pasture, sayeth the Lord.

God is watching every step we are taking in our lives; still people do not care about the creator, who created them in his own image.

Genesis 1:25-28: because of God's mercy and love, people take advantage to do whatever they want to do. Let me tell you, the final day is coming. It will be heaven or hell for all those who reject me, Jesus. There will be no mercy after death, because there is no repentance in the grave. So, do it now while you have a chance to turn your lives to God and serve him in humbleness of hearts.

Because of the love of me, Jesus, I came into this satanic world to rescue you from going to hell. I did not come to die for this world for nothing. I came that they might have life and have it more abundantly.

I came for you to do a simple thing, and that is to repent.

Mark 1:15: the time is fulfilled, and the kingdom of God is at hand. Repent ye and believe the gospel.

Change your ways and follow me, and I will make you fishers of men. The greatest of all is to have eternal life.

The book of Ezekiel 18:1-20 speaks about father not standing for the son; neither a son stands for his father. Wake up to do something for your soul. What is a man profiteth if he shall gain the whole world and lose his own soul. Matthew 16:26.

Once more I am appealing to this generation to come, for my coming is very near and no one knows the time and the hour, except my father. The new generation is coming. Christ will rule for 1,000 years, and then Satan will be bound for 1,000 years.

For unto us a child is born, and the government will be upon his shoulders. Jesus is the only one today who will bring peace into this world.

World leaders cannot solve the numerous problems the world is facing today. Technology has taken over the world and people take no heed that one day they are going to die and face the judgment seat of Jesus Christ.

St. John 3:16-17: for God so loved the world that he gave his only begotten son, that whosoever believeth in him should not perish, but have everlasting life. For God sent his son into the world not to condemn, but that the world through him be saved.

People have no time just to pray a simple prayer to my father and your father. The whole world is full of corruption, and my father is very sad that he created humans beings into this world to mess up his creation. No one appreciates God's wonderful creation.

I am still in the world, calling people to come and find rest for their weary souls.

Isaiah 59:1-2: behold, the Lord's hand is not shortened, that it cannot save; neither his heart heavy that it cannot hear.

Wake up children, and come to the Lord before it is too late.

I warned you all earlier that I would come like a thief in the night, and then it will be too late for you all.

Joshua 24:15: and if it seems evil unto you to serve the Lord, choose you this day whom ye will serve, whether the Gods which your fathers served that were on the other side of the flood, or the Gods of the Amorites, in whose land ye dwell; but as for me and my house, we will serve the Lord. The children of Israel suffered because of their stubbornness. They worship other Gods instead of the true and living God of Abraham, Isaac and Jacob. He came to his own and his own rejected him.

Those who accept him are children of the most high God, Sam. Keeps the good work going? Always preach me.

Bye, bye,

Jesus of Nazareth.

# Super Sunday—March 15, 2015

## I AM THE RESURRECTION AND THE LIFE

St. John 11:25: Jesus said unto her, I am the resurrection and the life. He that believeth in me, though he was dead, yet shall ye lives.

Jesus said unto Lisa, your brother shall rise again. Let us go, and show me the place.

St. John 11:35: Jesus wept; and when they arrived at the place, Jesus stood there and watched what he should do. The first thing was he gave thanks to the father in heaven, and said, "I know you always hear me, but because of these unbelievers around, let Lazarus come out of the grave, at once."

Jesus then said "Lazarus, come out," and the dead arose and came up. Everyone marveled.

He is a God of the living, not of the dead.

When he appeared to Moses, he appeared with a silent sound, and he said, "Moses removes your shoes, because the place where you are standing is holy ground." Moses obeyed the Lord. It was time for Moses to lead the children of Israel, to be delivered from the hands of pharaoh where they were in bondage for 450 years.

God prepared Moses for the journey. He, Jesus, told Moses, I am the God of Abraham, Isaac and Jacob, and I have chosen you to lead my people out of bondage to the promised land. A lot of miracles were done on the journey, but still the children of Israel doubted God. Many of them did not reach the promised land.

Moses missed the promised land, because he made a big mistake. Instead of talking to the rock, he struck the rock three times before the water came out. God wanted to be glorified in front of the people to let them know that he, God, was the one who was leading them to the promised land as he had promised.

This teaches us a lesson. When God speaks to us, as children of his, we must listen carefully before we act.

Jesus did a lot of wonderful things, but still people refuse to obey.

*Monday—March 16, 2015*

## THE NARROW PATH AND THE MIDDLETOWN BROAD WAY

Matthew 7:13-14: enter ye at the strait gate, for wide is the gate, and broad is the way that leadeth to destruction, and many there go in thereat; because strait is the gate, and narrow is the way, which leadeth unto life, and few there find it.

Narrow is the way that leads to eternal life on that road. There is persecution, strife, hardship and battling with the enemies. It is a very difficult way to walk into the kingdom of God, but those who endure to the end that are saved will enter in through the narrow path. Make up your minds, and choose the narrow path. It is the only way to enter into the kingdom of God. On the broad way, many people are heading that way, but it will lead to destruction of the soul

What does it profit a man to gain the whole world, and lose his own soul? Christ came to rescue us from dying in our sins.

Romans 3:23: for all have sinned, and come short of the glory of God. Jesus is calling you to come. Jesus is the only way to the kingdom of God.

St. John 14:6: I am the way, the truth and the life; no man cometh unto the father, but by me.

Therefore, choose the way you like. Either you are on the Lord's side, or the physical world which is the broad way.

I am with you, Sam. I will increase your knowledge about me. You are a chosen vessel for me. Go and preach hard to all generations. You are to carry on where the apostle Paul left off. You are writing for the new generation.

Matthew 28:18-20: and Jesus came and space unto them, saying, all power is given unto me in heaven and in earth. Go ye, therefore, and teach all nations, baptizing them in the name of the father, and of the son and of the Holy Ghost.

I will come and solve all the problems in the world very soon.

I am in the world, but people cannot see me because I am a spirit, and no more in the physical flesh. From the beginning was the word, and I came and dwelt among you for 33 and a half years. I said at the end I will pour out my spirit upon all flesh. I am the first and the last. Everyone belongs to me in this beautiful world my father created. I am coming to rule the world and my second coming is just around the corner. The word of God is powerful like a two-edged sword, piercing through the body.

Heaven and earth shall pass away, but my word shall not pass away.

The new commandment, I said unto you, love one another as I love you and died for you, so you will have life and have it more abundantly.

The author and finisher of our faith is God. Sam is a holy man. There will be an accident at pep boys, around the corner, early Monday morning. Do not go there.

I have to leave.

Sam, continue to preach hard on people to change their life styles. End of mission.

Jesus of Nazareth.

The next morning he saw a fig tree, and he wanted to have some of the fruits, and the tree looked good. But there was no fruit on the tree, so he, Jesus, cursed the fig tree to the ground. The real meaning of St. John 15:2-3: every branch in me that beareth not fruit he taketh away, and every branch that beareth fruit, he purged it, that it may bring forth more fruit. Now ye are clean through the word which I have spoken unto you.

Revelation 22:12-13: and behold I come quickly; and my reward is with me to give every man according as his works shall be. I am alpha and omega, the beginning and the end, the first and the last.

Each and every one will have to stand for themselves at the judgment seat of Christ, and he will be the judge.

In the book of St. John 3:16: for God so loved the world that he gave his only begotten son, that whosoever believeth in him should not perish, but have everlasting life.

Preach the word, Sam. Continue the good work for me. Bye, bye,

Jesus of Nazareth.

Psalms 44:4-5; psalms 104; psalms 102; psalms 105:1-15

## Wednesday—March 18, 2015

### A RIVER FLOWING WITH THE WATER OF LIFE

And when he, Jesus, entered into the river Jordan, he asked john to baptize him, but he refused and he said, do it in order that the bible would be fulfilled. It was 700 years ago that Isaiah prophesied about Jesus coming, and this is to bear record of john.

Jesus sent priests and Levites from Jerusalem to ask, who art thou? And he denied not, but confessed that I am not the Christ. He said, I am the voice of one crying in the wilderness. Make straight the way of the Lord.

The Lamb of God, which takes away the sins of the world and the government, shall be upon his shoulders. John bore record, saying, I saw the spirit descending from heaven like a dove and it abode upon him. I, john, saw and bear record that he is the son of God. The Holy Ghost's power came down from heaven upon him.

Jesus started his ministry with repentance. St Mark 1:15: he said, the kingdom of God is at hand. Repent you, therefore, and turn from your ways and follow me, and I will make you fishers of men. Jesus is calling each and every one to come to him so that they will have eternal life. I am standing at the door of your heart and when you open your heart, I will come in to you and sup with you.

The river flowing with water is the water of life, which is Jesus. He said unto the woman at Jacob's well, give me to drink? His disciples were gone into the city to buy meat. When Jesus asked the woman to give him to drink, she said she had no cup to fetch water. Jesus said to her, if thou knowest the gift of the Lord and whom sayeth to give thee to drink, then you would ask of him, and he would have given thee "living water". Jesus said anyone who drinks this water

That he shall give him, shall be a well of living water springing up into everlasting life; the word of God.

The woman ran to the village to tell to the elders, come, and see a man who was able to tell me all things. Jesus said to the Samaritan woman, who was a prostitute, if you only knew the gift that God has for you.

Glory hallelujah. Oh yes, he came for sinners to repent and have eternal life. He said to zacchaeus, come down from the sycamore tree, for today I am going to your house, for salvation has come to your house today.

## Thursday—March 19, 2015

### THE FAREWELL OF MOSES

The Lord appointed Joshua, the son of nun, to lead the children of Israel to the promised land. Moses was 120 years old when he died; his eye was not dim. Deut. 34:7.

Joshua 1:8-9: this book of the law shall not depart out of thy mouth; but thou shall meditate therein day and night, that thou mayest observe to do according to all that is written therein; for then thou shalt make the way prosperous, and then thou shalt have good success.

Joshua took over the leadership and led the children of Israel to the promised land. There were many obstacles, but they were able to conquer all through the wilderness.

The Lord directed Joshua what to do when they reached the wall of Jericho. They should go around the wall seven times, and then blow the trumpet and the wall would fall down. Then the children will cross over to the other side, which is the river Jordan, to possess the land promised to Abraham, Isaac and Jacob.

The children of Israel said unto Joshua, truly the Lord has delivered us into the land of our inheritance.

Joshua told the children of Israel to sanctify themselves, for tomorrow the Lord will do wonders among you.

Joshua 3:14-17: and it came to pass, when the people removed from their tents to pass over Jordan, and the priest bearing the ark of the covenant before the people; and as they that bare the ark were come unto Jordan, and the feet of the priests that bare the ark were dipped in the brim of the water, for Jordan overfloweth all his banks at the time of harvest. That the waters which came down from above stood and rose up as heap very far from the city. Adam that is beside zaretan; and those that came down towards the sea of the plain even the salt sea failed and were cut off; and the people passed over right against Jericho. And the priest that bare the ark of the covenant of the Lord stood firm on dry ground in the midst of Jordan, and all the Israelites passed over on dry ground until all the people were passed clean over Jordan.

After he was resurrected on the third day, he came to the disciples and said to them, all power have been given to me, both heaven and earth. Go therefore and make new disciples, teaching them to observe all things which I have spoked unto you, baptizing them in the name of the father, the son and the Holy Spirit. And Lord, I am with you always, even unto the end of the world.

Amen.

## Thursday—March 19, 2015

St. John 8:32: and we shall know the truth, and the truth shall make you free. The Lord Jesus Christ came into this world to declare the truth of the gospel, and he did exactly what the father asked him to do, and yet we sent him to the cross because of the truth. The truth brought him to life from the grave. The purpose of his coming was only one thing: to declare the gospel in common language.

St. John 3:16-17: the spirit of the truth is Jesus. Jesus said what wrong have I done that you are stoning me? Is it because of the good works that I have done, or because I speak the truth of my father. The only way to enter into the kingdom of God is if the truth is in you. No hatred. Love your neighbor as yourself, and thou shall love the Lord thy God with all your mind, soul, body and strength.

From the beginning God created Adam and eve. Eve is the one who disobeyed God's commandments. The Holy Spirit is the spirit of truth. Acts 1:1-4: the holy aims to declare the truth of the gospel. St. John 1:1-5:

The gospel is the truth of God talking to mankind. He uses common people like Sam to write the book with the power from above with the inspiration of the Holy Spirit.

The law was given to Moses, but grace and mercy was given to Jesus Christ. Jesus said I am the resurrection and the life; he that believeth in me, though he was dead, yet shall he lives.

Sam's heart's desire is to preach the word to win souls for the kingdom of God. The world is now going crazy about technology, but one day everything will come to an end and it will be sooner than they expect.

Bye, bye, Sam, Jesus of Nazareth.

# GOD DEMONSTRATES HIS LOVE TO US

In the garden of gethsemane, that very hour, he told his father that the cup was too heavy to bear that was leading to the death of Jesus on the cross. Sam, I am revealing these things to you because you are a faithful servant in doing my work.

Do not worry about anything that is happening, because I am with you everywhere you go. There is a lot of temptation in the world. Some people are wondering about you. They have heard about the anointing upon you. Be careful. Do not go around them. Invitations will be coming from the churches. Do not go to the African church. I am not there. It is all about money and nothing else.

You preach directly from the bible. That is why my father loves you. Sam does not add or subtract. Revelation 22:19: continue to preach the truth of the gospel. Deuteronomy 28:1-10.

More people will be joining the Lord's bible studies in the near future. The Australia tour will happen in the near future. You will be preaching all over the world.

Matthew 28:18-20: your anointing is very powerful. You suffered a long time for this blessing. Just be careful. There are a lot of funny preachers out there.

Corinthians 1:9: God is faithful, by whom ye were called unto fellowship of the son Jesus our Lord.

You have more strength; more than those who are sleeping. The angels are at all times at this apartment, 15e.

The end of my visit.

Bye, bye,

Jesus Christ of Nazareth.

## Friday—March 20, 2015

### "EVEN THE SEA AND THE WIND OBEY HIM."

Matthew 8:20-27: and Jesus sayeth unto him, the foxes have holes, and the birds of the air have nests, but the son of man hath nowhere to lay his head.

And one of the disciples said to him, Lord, suffer me first to go and bury my father. But Jesus said to him; let the dead bury the dead. And they were at sea, in the boarding at the back of the ship when a heavy wind blew, and the sea began to get rough and they were afraid. They called out to Jesus and told him about the tempest and the wind, and he woke up and rebuked the wind and the sea became calm. And the disciples said what man is this, that even the wind obeyed him. Yes, they were walking with him for 3 and half years, but they did not know him, because they were not in the spirit, but in the flesh, and the flesh profiteth nothing, but the spirit quickeneth. St. John 6:63:

He said, "The words I speak unto you are life." Jesus said, "no one goes to my father, only through me, Thomas. Lord, you leaving us lonely, but we don't know the way." Jesus said, "Do you know that I am the way, the truth, and the life. The words I speak unto you, they are life."

I am going to mine and your father, and he will send the Holy Spirit to you that the work I left behind, you must continue.

And they were in the upper room with one accord singing and praising God when the Holy Spirit came upon them.

I am coming with iron hands to rule the world, and that will be my second coming with horses and chariots.

I walked on the sea to demonstrate the power of the almighty God. Peter also walked on the sea, but the very hour he took his eyes off Jesus he began to sink.

Sam is faithfully performing his daily duties. His writings have been signature by me, Jesus Christ. Sam did not call himself. I called him. He will do many wonderful things in my name. God is good to those who sincerely love him from their heart. The bible says, thou shall love the Lord thy God with our heart, your mind and soul. For we all have to face the judgement seat and I, Jesus, will reward every man according to the works they do for me.

Jeresophiah 23:1: woe be unto the pastors that destroy and scatter the sheep of my pasture, sayeth the Lord.

Be patient with some of the members; don't let them go away.

The Holy Communion services on Sundays are not a church. Teach and preach me Jesus, the author and finisher of our faith. Without faith it is impossible to please God. By faith my father created the world.

Genesis 1:10: and God called the dry land earth; and the gathering together of the waters he called seas; and God saw that it was good.

Amen.

SAM, I HAVE TO GO. BYE, BYE FOR NOW. JESUS OF NAZARETH.

## Wednesday—March 25, 2015

### CHRIST SERMON TO THE PEOPLE

Isaiah 55:1-4: ho, every one that is thirsteth, come ye to the waters, and he that hath no money, come ye, buy and eat. Yea, come buy wine and milk without money and without price.

Hebrews 13:8: Jesus Christ is the same yesterday, today and forever.

And it came to pass that as he was praying in a crowded place and when he had ceased praying, one of the disciples said unto him, Lord, teach us how pray as john also taught his disciples. And he said to them, when you pray say St. Luke 11:2: "our father, which art in heaven, hallowed be thy name, and he said to them, which of you shall have a friend and shall go out at midnight and say unto him, "friend, lend me three loaves of bread for a friend of mine who has journeyed to me and I have nothing to set before him."

Isaiah 59:1-2: behold, the Lord's hand is not shortened, that it cannot save.

Neither his ear heavy, that it cannot hear. Then why did not God answer our prayer, it is because of our iniquities?

Proverbs 28:13: he that covereth his sins shall not prosper. 1 john 1:8-9: if we say we have no sin, we deceive ourselves.

God is holy; we must be holy to come to him with our prayers. The body is the temple of God. Keep it holy.

Exodus 3: and God said to Moses; take your shoes from your feet, because the place where you are standing is holy ground. How can you expect God to answer your prayer without holiness? It is not just a matter of prayers, but how to keep yourself before coming to me, Jesus. God is holy; therefore you must be holy before coming to me for prayers. I also fasted often when I was in the world, because the devil is busy in the world. He has poison in which to get people. He comes to destroy and to kill. He is going around like a roaring lion wanting to destroy people. In my first sermon in galilee, I said, the time is fulfilled, and the kingdom of God is at hand. Repent ye and believe the gospel.

Matthew 11:28: come unto me, all ye that labor and are heavy laden, and I will give you rest.

The golden gate. Matthew 7:13: enter ye in at the strait gate, for wide is the gate and broad is the way that leadeth to destruction, and many there be which go in thereat; because strait is the gate and narrow is the way, which leadeth unto life, and few there be that find it.

In the narrow path there is much suffering, but at the end you will have eternal life. I am the only way to the father.

St. John 14:6: I am the way, the truth and the life.no man cometh unto the father, but by me.

John 3:1-21: there was a man of the Pharisees named nicodemus, a ruler of the Jews. The same came to Jesus by night and said unto him rabbi, we know that thou art a teacher come from God; for no man can do these miracles that thou doest except God be with him.

St. John 6:1-13: Jesus performed the miracle with the five barley loaves and the two small fishes.

The miracle was performed at the wedding feast where he turned water into wine. During the next miracle, the woman with the issue of blood, Jacob's well, walking on the Sea of Galilee, healing the sick, bringing Lazarus to life. The women who visited the tomb early morning... Matthew 28:1-10.

A miracle of the resurrection of life. He that believeth in me, tho he was dead yet shall he lives. Glory hallelujah. Amen. Revelation 22:12-13.

Revelation 22:19-20.

Amen. Sam, I am leaving. I will return. Good bye.

The second book should come out in June, 2016.

Jesus himself showed me the time. God is real. One day after finishing prayers, he asked me to go to the computer. This was the opening of the way to go to the worldwide Christian center in Israel.

The Lord appears to me every day. I am still writing. He says Apostle Paul write in the prison, but I, Sam, is writing outside the prison.

They are all planning to kill you, but I always will guide and protect you. No weapon that is formed against you shall prosper. You are my servant to preach me, Jesus.

Revelation 22:11: he that is unjust, let him be unjust still, and he that is filthy, let him be filthy still, and he that is righteous, let him be righteous still, and he that is holy, let him be holy still.

Revelation 22:12: behold, I come quickly and my reward is with me to give every man according as his work shall be.

Glory be to God almighty, the creator of heaven and earth. Amen. Jesus of Nazareth.

Good bye, Sam.

## Thursday—March 26, 2015

You cannot understand God. Don t you know he is God of good and will give punishment to you, too? He is standing at your door and knocking. You are nothing; only like a flower in the morning. It bloometh beautifully and in the night it fadeth.

You see how the wind blows. Human beings are like that. You see us today, but you do not know tomorrow what it brings. Matthew 6:33-34.

God provided everything for us; just believe. People will question why they have to believe, but that is not the end. There is more beyond death. If there is nothing after death, why should I come from heaven to die and shed my blood to save mankind? If you do not open your heart to me, I will not come in. St. John 14:6: Jesus sayeth unto him, I am the way, the truth and the life; no man cometh unto the father, but by me. I am the only way to the father. There's no better place than heaven. It is a beautiful place, but unless you live a holy life, you cannot enter there.

You cannot live in the flesh and do whatever you want to do and go to heaven. I said if you love me, keep my commandments. Do you really love God? The you should do what he asks.

Exodus 20:4-6: thou shalt have no other gods before me. Tho art not make unto thee any graven image, or any likeness of anything that is in heaven or that is in the earth, beneath, or that is in the water under the earth.

Do not fool around. God knows everything about you.

Sam is not better than anybody, but he loves God and he is always ready to work for me. He likes to preach. That is why I called him back from death to life to do my work; a very faithful man. When he is sleeping he wakes up to write about me. The glasses were next behind me Sam, but I did not see it until I was almost finish writing. All is to prove that I am still alive and working in the lives of my chosen ones.

I am the first and the last. I have the key to both heaven and hell. There will be no repentance, no kingdom for you.

If there is a resurrection, then one should die and come to life again once he or she believes in me.

St. John 11:25-36: Jesus said unto her, I am the resurrection and the life. He that believeth in me, though he were dead, yet shall he live, and whosoever liveth and believeth in me shall never die. Believest thou this?

I am the bread of life to the whole world. Either believe it or not. There is hell. It is not a place to go. All you have to do is accept me as your personal savior and live a holy life to enter into the kingdom.

*Friday—March 27, 2015*

## "I AM THE ROUGH SEA AT GALILEE."
## MATTHEW 8:24

And behold, there arose a great tempest in the sea, insomuch that the ship was covered with the waves; but he was asleep.

And even the sea obeyed him. They were at sea when the sea thundered to bring heavy waves. And behold there arose a great storm in the sea. The ship was covered with waves. He, Jesus, was asleep, and the disciples came and woke him, saying, and "Lord, save us. We perish." And he said unto them, "Why are you afraid, you of faith?" Then he arose and rebuked the winds and the sea. Then there was a great calm. The men marveled, saying, "What manner of man is this that even the winds and the sea obeyed him? It must be the Christ, the savior of the world, the holy one of Israel. That is the one john spoke about.

St. John. 1:29: the next day john saw Jesus coming unto him and said, "Behold the lamb of God which takes away the sins of the world. This is the one of whom I said after me cometh a man, which is preferred before me, and I knew him not, but he that sent me. Therefore, I am baptizing you with water." And john bore witness, saying," I saw the spirit descending from heaven like a dove, and it abode upon him. Praise the Lord, thy God of heaven, the mighty one of

Israel, the impossible one of Abraham, Isaac and Jacob the foundation of the world. If you do not know him, you must know that he is the savior of the world. He that sent me to baptize with water, the same said to me, upon whom thou shall see the spirit descending and remaining on him, the same is he, who baptize with the Holy Ghost."

Again, the next day after, john stood and two of his disciples heard him speak, and they followed him, Jesus.

St. John 1:38-39: then Jesus turned and saw them following, and sayeth unto them, "what seek ye?"

They said unto him. "Rabbi, which is interpreted, master, where dwells thou?" And he said, "come," and where he dwelt and they abode with him that day for it was about the tenth hour.

Sam, a big reward is waiting for you in heaven. Do not change your phone number, because people will be calling you for prayers and healing mentally, etc.

Matthew 11-28:30: come unto me, all ye that labor and are heavy laden, and I will give you rest.

Sanctify the Lord God in your hearts.

1 peter 3:15: but sanctify the Lord God in your hearts, and be ready always to give an answer to every man that asketh you a reason of the hope that is in you with meekness and fear.

The apostle Paul.

Corinthians 2:2: for I determined not to know anything among you, save Jesus Christ, and him I crucified.

That should be our intentions as Christians, to only mind the thing pertaining to Jesus Christ.

God bless you, Sam. Jesus of Nazareth.

## Thursday—March 26, 2015

Revelation 3:20: behold, I stand at the door and knock; if any man hear my voice, and open the door, I will come in to him, and will sup with him, and he with me. How can I enter if you close the door on me? It is impossible to enter the kingdom of God without a key to heaven or hell. I am the only one who has the authority to open and close the door. Human beings have closed their hearts to me, and they go around praying for results. I preached repentance, "sleep and wake up to write," but they ignored my teachings. It is impossible to please God without faith.

Genesis 12:1-25: the Lord had said unto Abram, get thee out of thy country, and from thy kindred, and from thy father's house, unto a land that I will show thee.

When I called Abram, he left everything behind and obeyed my commandments to go. That is the reason why he has the blessing from me. Travelling to Egypt is a blessing in disguise. It is better to listen to the bible (word) from the beginning, and the word became flesh and dwelt among us. It is better to listen; obedience is better than sacrifice.

Sam is doing a good job listening to me. I am the only way to heaven. I came from heaven. Therefore, examine yourself carefully. I, Jesus, am the one who started the music, like the hymns of praises in the prayer room. I am always there. God is good to all those who love him, and I chose Sam to work for me, because he is a very humble person. I will also open the door for everyone to enter into the kingdom if only you listen to my preaching.

People, the word are everything. The world was founded by the word. Sam, continue to read more about me. In the spirit, your trip will be successful.

Wonderful things will happen. The whole world is coming, different churches and different people. It is an honor for both of you, Sam and dorthula. Your reward is awaiting you.

There is no respect in the world today; it has become so corrupt; more evil than good. Don't you know that the world is coming to an end very soon because of corruption?

St. John 3:16: for God so loved the world that he gave his only begotten son, that whosoever believeth in him should not perish, but have everlasting life. Satan has gotten ahold of their lives, because they do not know me, and have never made up their minds to know me. No one is going to live forever. After death comes the judgement. People think it is a joke, but it is real. The kingdom is real. Therefore, hell is also real. There would not be heaven without hell. That's how my father designed it.

It was God who created you in his image. Breathe the breath of life into your body and you become a living soul. The world is full of surprises, and no one can imagine that. Just believe that with God all things are possible.

## Thursday—March 26, 2015

My love for you, Sam, is the reason why I brought you back from darkness eleven and a half years ago. You are dead body walking on this satanic world. You suffer for my sake. Now I have put light upon you, that wherever you go the light of me is showing. Things happen for a reason. Now everybody knows the purpose of your sickness. They plan together to kill you, but they cannot. I am with you as I promised in Matthew 28:18-20: all power is given unto me in heaven and in earth. Go ye, therefore, and teach all nations, baptizing them in the name of the father and of the son, and of the holy ghost, teaching them to observe all things whatsoever I have commanded you; and Lord, I am with you always, even unto the end of the world. Amen.

Sam, preach the word. The wisdom has been given to you already, go and preach the words for people to receive salvation, those who are in darkness so that they will turn from their wicked ways to come to me, Jesus.

God is talking through his servant. Some in the family doubts you, because they still live in darkness. They are jealous of you and talk about you, Sam. Just because I gave you a car they are envious of you. The family was not expecting you would have such a beautiful car. It is a gift from me to you, Sam. Your spiritual sickness cannot be compared to physical sickness.

Don't you see, everywhere you go people like you. I did miracles so more people who would come to listen to your messages, and also for them to see how I am working through you.

St. John 14:12-12: believest thou not that I am in the father, and the father in me? The words that I speak unto you I speak not of myself, but the father that dwelleth in me. He doeth the work.

I, Jesus, call those whom I love to write for me. People are now guessing about you, Sam, in the family. They still cannot believe what has happened to you. Your spirit will overcome any other that is not of your spirit. A person who is in the flesh cannot compete with one who is in the spirit. You Sam are fully anointed by God to do his work. Sam, never add or subtract. Revelation 22:19.

Continue with Isaiah 53:4-5: for the holy communion services. On the trip take pictures to come and show to people and to the members of the Lord's bible studies.

## Thursday—March 26, 2015

In the beginning God created the heaven and the earth, and the earth was without form. Darkness was upon the face of the earth. And the spirit of God moved upon the face of the earth. He saw the light, and said it was good. Then he divided the light from the darkness. If God knows that light was better than darkness, why is it that some human beings love the darkness? It is because the devil is the ruler of darkness. He has blinded the minds of them. Therefore they have no fear of God. Jesus said, I am the light of the world, and he came from heaven to show the world that living in darkness brings separation from God.

When one enters into a dark room what do you do? You put the lights on so you can see clearly. My reason for coming into the world is to show the light of God. Those who live in darkness do the things of the darkness, and there is no light in them. The light of the universe is Jesus. In the book of psalms David said, where shall I go from your presence? If I make my bed in hell thou art there, if I say the darkness shall cover thee the night shall be light about me. Because you are the light of the world, wherever you are I am seeing you. There is no hiding place where I will not see you.

The love you have for me is good and powerful. The Lord's studies are a blessed organization, because Sam is a very good person and one who loves the Lord. God is very happy with Sam and dorthula. Sam has suffered so much in this world. Now is a time for him to enjoy life. Dorthula is always thinking backward.

Sam loves Stephanie so much as his own daughter. Sometimes when he remembers her he cries a lot. I healed Sam to do my work. I would not have any good person to do my work. He is a very peculiar person who loves the word, (the bible). He does not add or subtract from the holy word. Can't you people see that Sam is a changed person? Every time you see him, he is always speaking about me, Jesus. How can a person do this without the Holy Spirit? Open your eyes to see things. I woke him up at 5:00 a.m. to come and write about me for the future. Sam is always ready for my call, very humble and clever. He has gone through a lot in his life. His father died when he was only 13 years old, and his mother also died when he was 16 years old. He tried his best to finish school. Now, Sam has nobody but me, Jesus.

If Sam says do not join a church, it means you have to listen to him. Apartment 15e is blessed and a special place for me to dwell. Everything is in order.

Sam, be careful. Some people do not like you because of your anointing, but they cannot harm you. As I say, I am always with you. They want to kill you for your blessings, but they cannot. They cannot suffer as you do for your blessings. They are partakers of the worldly things, like going to parties and their holidays. God is not sleeping; the world is. These people have no time for the creator. Technology has taken over the whole world and they are all about it, but a day is coming soon when technology will fail and the end will come. The end will be worse than

Sodom and Gomorrah. People are presently destroying their bodies because of money. Sexual behavior is taking over this satanic world, because the devil is using them to behave in this ungodly way.

Christians have to be very careful about me, Jesus. Otherwise, punishment will come to them and they would lose their blessings from heaven. People in the world are sleeping instead of praying.

Sam is very clever. He always remembers what the consequences were during his time of spiritual sickness. Always happy in the world and always thanking God.

Sam is a good leader. He would give his last dollar. That is the person I want to work for me.

Sam is a good teacher of the bible, he is always reading about me. Jesus of Nazareth.

Sam loves to preach. That is why I called him back from death to life again. Love my organization "the Lord's bible studies".

Bye, bye,

Jesus of Nazareth.

## Friday—April 17, 2015

St. John 14:6: Jesus sayeth, I am the way, the truth and the life. No man cometh unto the father, but by me.

How can you go to a place without knowing the way? At least you have to ask someone who knows the place to lead you to. I came to the world to lead people to the kingdom of God, because I came from there, and I know the place very well. That is where I was created before coming into the world. I came and sacrificed for mankind, and demonstrated miracles for the world to see and know that I came from the father above.

The miracles I perform are not from me, they are from my father, and he gave me the power to raise Lazarus from the dead. I prayed to my father because I have no power to raise a dead body, but my father can. He said, "Roll the away," but Lisa said," Lord, by now he stinketh. It will be terrible, because he has been dead for four days."

St. John 11:37: and some of them said, could not this man, which opened the eyes of the blind, have cause that even this man should not have died?

Broad is the way that leads to destruction, which is hell. The narrow gate leads to life eternal and the only way in which to enter into the kingdom of God, and few there be who finds it.

Choose this day which way you will enter into hell or heaven?

St. Mark 1:15: the time is fulfilled, and the kingdom of God is at hand. Repent ye, and believe the gospel.

Bye, bye,

Jesus of Nazareth.

# April 15, 2015

## "I AM THE LIGHT OF THE WORLD."

St. John 8:12: then spake Jesus again unto them, saying, I am the light of the world; he that followeth me shall not walk in darkness, but shall have the light of life.

Meeting Jesus is the first step in a journey that is filled with struggles as well as blessings, with temptations, sickness and even sometimes death, but always continue to the end. All Christians must believe his word.

St. John 8:10: when Jesus had lifted up himself, and saw none but the woman, he said unto her, woman, where are those accusers? Hath no man condemned thee?

This woman was caught in the act of adultery. Under the Law of Moses they were supposed to stone her to death when caught in the act. What do you say to this? When Jesus asked, "Where are thine accusers?" She said, "No man, Lord." Jesus said unto her, "neither do I condemn thee. Go and sin no more."

Jesus spoke unto the crowd again, saying, I am the light of the world. He that followeth me shall not walk in darkness, but shall have life. The Pharisees said, you are making false claims about yourself. The record is not true.

St. John 8:14: Jesus answered and said unto them, though I bear record of myself, yet my record is true. For I know whence I came and whither I go, but ye cannot tell whence I come, and whither I go."

Yes, my record is true to continue to the end.

And if I judge, my judgements are true, for I am not alone, but I am of the father who sent me.

Then he said again unto them, whither I go ye cannot come.

I am the light of the world that comes upon every human being on earth. I came from the father.

Genesis 1:4: and God saw the light, that it was good; and God divided the light from the darkness.

Isaiah 40:27-31: why sayest thou, 0 Jacob, and speakest 0 Israel. My way is hidden from the Lord, and my judgement is passed over from my God.

Psalms 139:7-12: whither shall I go from thy spirit? Or whither shall I flee from thy presence? If I ascend up into heaven, thou art there. If I make my bed in hell, behold thou art there.

Again he said, "I am the light of the world, and there is no darkness around me. Keep yourself holy unto me. Your body is the temple of God. Keep it holy. No one can enter into the kingdom without being holy. I came that you must see light, not electricity. I am the light that lighteth everyone's path. God is good.

Revelation 22:7: behold, I come quickly. Blessed is he that keepeth the sayings of the prophecy of this book.

I am alpha and omega, the beginning and the end, the first and the last. I have to leave the body now.

Bye, bye,

Sam

Preach me, Jesus, the author and finisher of your faith.

God bless you.

## April 19, 2015

### "THE DEVIL" PSALMS 139:4-5: PSALMS 61:8

Sam, continue the good works. The devil will attack you wherever you go, because of me. Your own household will go against you, but do not worry. I am with you always.

Watch and see the end results of them from me, Jesus.

The devil wants to put you to shame through them, but they will suffer.

Do not worry. The organization is growing, and I will see to it that it grows worldwide. Sam, you are on the right path. That is why the devil is mad at you, because you are always in the spirit. The end of everything is coming very soon, and I am on your side. No one can harm you. Instead, they should be careful about you, Sam. They should read the word of God (the bible).

Exodus 20:6: and showing mercy unto thousands of them that love me, and keep my commandment.

No respect for me. We will see the end of everyone.

More blessings are coming to you, Sam. I brought you back to work after your long spiritual sickness. You have a good heart and you love God. My father loves you so much. No weapon that is formed against thee shall prosper, and every tongue that shall rise against thee in judgement thou shall condemn. This is the heritage of the servants of the Lord, and their righteousness is of me, sayeth the Lord.

The devil is using your own people to bring you down, but they would rather be down themselves. They have no holy spirit in them.

Yes Sam, you know the word, which is the scriptures, because I have put it in your mouth and in your brain.

Just watch and pray, Sam., I will do the rest. It is because of me, Jesus, why all this is happening to you.

The car is your reward for suffering for 11 and half years. You open your heart to help a lot of people, but they forsake you. Just be happy, Sam.

He said, he is the voice crying in the wilderness. Prepare ye the way for the Lord's coming. Making straight the road for him. Baptism of Jesus.

St. John 1:33: and I knew him not, but he that sent me to baptize with water, the same said unto me, upon whom thou shalt see the spirit descending, and remaining on him, the same he which baptized with the holy ghost.

Then Jesus went from galilee to the river Jordan to be baptized by john, but john did not want to baptize Jesus. John said, "I am the one who needs to be baptized by you, Jesus. Why are you coming to me to baptize you?" Jesus answered and said, "It must be done, because he must do everything that is right."

John bore record, saying, I saw the spirit descending from heaven like a dove, and it abode upon him, and lo, a voice saying, this is my beloved son, in whom I am well pleased.

Matthew 4:1: then was Jesus led out into the wilderness by the Holy Spirit to be tempted of the devil for forty days and nights. He ate nothing and was very ill. The devil then came to him and said to him, if you are the son of God. Kneed these stones into bread, but Jesus said to him, people need more than bread for their lives. They must be fed with the word of God. I am he that sends the angels to protect you, and they will hold you with their hands to keep you from striking your foot against a stone. The scripture also says, do not tempt the Lord your God.

As Jesus Christ was tempted, so Christians will also be tempted. Be careful. The devil is very crafty. He is just waiting to get whom he can devour. His job is to steal, kill and destroy.

St. Mark 1:16: now as he walked by the sea of galilee, he saw Simon Andrew, his brother, casting a net into the sea, for they were commercial fishermen. Jesus called out to them, come ye after me and I will make you become fishers of men.

I will show you how to fish for people, and they left their nets and followed him. Jesus is the way to the father.

Romans 8:28-30: and we know that all things work together for good to them that love God, to them who are called according to his purposes.

Bye for now, Jesus of Nazareth.

## *April 20, 2015*

### "I AM THE WAY TO THE FATHER."

St. John 14:6: I am the way, the truth and the life. No man cometh unto the father, but by me.

There is no other way than through me. I came to offer my whole life for mankind, and yet some do not regard me as the savior of the world.

Isaiah 9:16: for the leaders of this people cause them to err, and they that are led of them are destroyed.

Romans 8:25: but if we hope for that we see not, then do we with patience wait for it?

I led the disciples to show them the way. I said no one would go to the father, only by me. Take it or leave it, but the end thereof will be the death.

In my first sermon, I preached repentance. Mark 1:15: people in the world do not regard me as being the God of Abraham, Isaac and Jacob. I am standing at the door of your heart and knocking, but you refuse to open your heart for me enter in. Yes, I know what you are going to say. Is it a reality that the son of man can enter into you? Yes, he can, if you will let him in.

How about the free will my father gave to you? Yes, use it, but know that the end will tell. You better repent and change your lifestyles.

2 Corinthians 6:2: behold, now is the acceptable time. Behold, now is the day of salvation.

There will be fire and brimstone on that awful day. No time for repentance. It will be too late.

Isaiah 55:6: seek ye the Lord, while he may be found. Call ye upon him while he is near; praise be to the Lord.

I am always with you, Sam. You are a good person. When you say something you mean it. My father loves you so much because you listen whenever I talk to you. You stand by your word and change not.

Sam, how about the prophecy at the hospital? You declared it and it happened.

Sister Lisa should choose where to worship. She is only wasting her time, and under the leadership of someone whom I have not called to do my work. She should choose to be in the Lord's bible studies.

Sam is teaching the word. He never adds or subtracts. Revelation 22:19.

I am the word from the beginning of age, and the word became flesh and dwell among you. He came back to his own and his own rejected him, so that is why he, Jesus came to the gentiles.

Jesus suffered in the world because they rejected him. Everyone's blessings came to us because of father Abraham, some do not deserve it, but we were already blessed from generations of Abraham, Isaac and Jacob.

Even though Sam suffered so much for my sake, he still kept the faith in me. He never questions when I talk to him; he just listens.

Sam is qualified to do my work. That is why I called him. Dorthula should study Sam very well. I have prepared him for 11 and half years to continue the work I left behind.

You are doing a good job. My blessing be upon you, Sam, and the family. Jesus.

I am leaving now. Bye, bye, Sam.

# THIS I DECLARE OF THE LORD

Psalms 27:5: for in the time of trouble he shall hide me in his pavilion; in the secret of his tabernacle shall he hide me; he shall set me upon a rock.

Psalms 5:9: for there is no faithfulness in their mouth; their inward part is very wickedness; their throat is an open sepulcher, they flatter with their tongue.

Psalms 72:1: give the king thy judgements, Oh God, and thy righteousness unto the king's son.

Christians today in the world accept other religious appearances in the place of the real spirit of God. The promise of the Holy Spirit is given in the book of acts.

Acts 1:8: but ye shall receive power, after that the Holy Ghost is come upon you, and ye shall be witnesses unto me both in Jerusalem and in all Judaea, and in Samaria, and unto the uttermost part of the earth.

I have given you, Sam, prophet, preacher and writer. Three in one. Jesus speaking to me.

Sam, you are a good person. You have a good heart towards people. I like the way you present me, Jesus, to people. Everybody in the kingdom is proud of you. You will live for many years to proclaim my name everywhere.

Dorthula should have patience with you. You have suffered so long in your life since 1974 in the navy. Then 1987-2003, and recently the car accident at the garage. You called on my name, and I saved your life again from the accident, because you have a lot to do for me. Sam, you project me everywhere you go. People love you so much. As soon as they see you they are happy. I am always with you wherever you go. More blessings are coming to you. It is on the way.

Psalms 119:165: Great peaces have they which love thy law; and nothing shall offend them.

Continue to be humble as you are. That is your nature. I am watching everything going on in this apartment 15e. You are very patient about a lot of things. Continue your life the way you are going. People outside see more of you than those in the family. They did the same to me. Family is the first people to betray you. Do not worry. Continue the work I called you to do.

## Thursday—April 23, 2015

Matthew 5:12: rejoice and be exceedingly glad, for great is your reward in heaven; for so persecuted the prophets which were before you.

Revelation 22:12-13: and behold, I come quickly; and my reward is with me to give every man according as his works shall be. I am alpha and omega, the beginning and the end, the first and the last.

Sam, do not preach any other gospel except me, Jesus. My word is life and the spirit. I am the light of the world. My spirit shines on everyone who comes into this world.

1. I am the bread of life.
2. I am the resurrection and the life.
3. I am alpha and omega, the first and the last.
4. Noah's days will be coming soon/ my father is not pleased about the world.
5. Sam, pray more and more miracles will happen through you. I will always speak through you.
6. The spirit is upon you, and it is very powerful and strong.
7. We prepared you for this work you are doing.

I want a holy man to do my work. That is why you were sick for so many years. No more death in your household.

The light is coming. I have to go. Preach me, Jesus of Nazareth. The communion services are very good. I am always there.

Start communion service at 00 p.m. sharp. Abide with my command.

Bye, bye,

Jesus of Nazareth.

## Saturday—April 25, 2015

Isaiah 53:4-5: surely he hath borne our grieves and carried our sorrows; yet we did esteem him stricken, smitten of God, and afflicted, but he was wounded for our transgression. He was bruised for our inequities; the chastisement of our peace was upon him, and with his stripes we are healed.

The Lord's suffering servant will prosper. He will be highly exalted. Many were amazed when they saw him, Jesus, beaten and bloodied. He was so disfigured. One would wonder why he suffered like that, but it was all because he had to do the will of the father who sent him.

He was despised and rejected. He was wounded for our transgressions. It was our weakness. He carried our sorrows that weighed him down. People thought his punishment was from God, but he had to go through all this so that we should know his suffering and have eternal life.

Like sheep we have left God's path to follow our own ways of life. The Lord laid on him the guilt and sins of us all. He never opened his mouth to say anything. He was led as a lamb to be slaughtered, and then he was led away to his death. He did no wrong. He was buried in a rich man's tomb.

He bore the sins of us all and interceded for sinners.

God showed his great love for us by sending Jesus Christ to die for us.

Romans 5:8: but commendeth his love towards us in that while we were yet sinners, Christ died for us.

Jesus's great commandment was that we love our neighbors as ourselves. He also commanded us to love one another as I have loved you.

Love is not jealous, love does not brag, and is not arrogant, does not act unseemingly, is not easily provoked, but rejoices with the truth, bears all things, believes all things, endures all things. Love never fails.

What can separate us from the love of God? The love of God is universal. The end. Amen.

Bye, bye,

Jesus of Nazareth.

# I AM THE RESURRECTION AND THE LIFE

St. John 11:25: Jesus said unto her, I am the resurrection and the life; he that believeth in me, though he was dead, yet shall he lives.

The servant said unto him, Lord behold a man whom thou lovest is dead. Jesus said, it is not unto death, but for the glory of God. Death has no power over him, because he defeated the devil on the cross. Jesus proved to the whole world that he is the son of God.

He performed miracles when he walked on the Sea of Galilee, also at Canaan. He turned water into wine. People saw the miracle he performed, and they believed in him. People said, is he not the carpenter's son? He is not the son 0f the carpenter, but the son of the most high God. The bible said as many believed on him, he gave them power to become the children of God.

He raised the futile girl from the dead. Tell them to loose her, and give her water to drink.

The next day john saw him, Jesus, coming towards him and he said, look, there is the Lamb of God who takes away the sins of the world. And john bore record, saying, I saw the spirit descending from heaven like a dove, and abode upon him. St. John 1:34.

And I, john, saw and bore record, and looking upon Jesus as he walked.

And the disciples left everything and followed Jesus. And he, Jesus, said to them, why seekest thou? And he said unto them, come see where I dwellest. They followed Jesus and they stayed with him for a day.

It was about the tenth hour that the son of man came to this world as a child to bare our sins on the cross. For our sake, he was despised and rejected by men. Isaiah 53:4-5.

Those who follow that which is evil have not seen God. And Jesus said to Thomas, I am the way, the truth and the life.

Sam, it is getting to morning. I have to leave. Preach the good news about the kingdom of God and the spirit left me. Sam, I could not wait any longer.

Bye, bye,

Jesus of Nazareth.

Sunday—April 26, 2015

**THE ANGELS WAKE ME UP WITH MUSIC PLAYING.**

Matthew 2:1-2: now when Jesus was born in Bethlehem, Judea, in the days of herod the king, behold there came wise men to Jerusalem saying, where is he that is born king of the Jews, for we have seen his star in the east and come to worship him.

Isaiah 9:6: for unto us a child is born. Unto us a son is given and the government shall be upon his shoulder; and his name shall be called wonderful, counselor, the mighty God, the everlasting father, the Austin of peace.

He brought peace on earth when he was raised from the dead on the third day. He came to the disciples when they forced themselves in a room, and he, Jesus, said unto them, peace be with you. God did not send his son into the world to condemn, but through him the world might be saved. St. John 3:17

Jesus was born as the light of the world, but people love the darkness rather than the light, because their deeds are evil. Jesus, the light of the world.

God healed me and he bestowed his blessings upon me, Sam. What happened in Augusta, Georgia, at the wedding, November 7, 2014, it was there that I was called by him to start writing. My second writing was at a birthday gathering December 20, 2014. Ever since I have been writing every morning when he, Jesus, comes to call me.

He showed me a lot of wonderful things in the world about his suffering when he was a baby born in a manger. Jesus of Nazareth is a real person in the spirit visiting people whom he loves, and who do his will.

It is marvelous how God is using me, Sam, to preach the gospel as he said.

On September 18, 2014, he asked me to start bible studies in the apartment 15e. And that he, Sam, should name it "the Lord's bible studies". In a short time the number increased to 16 members. He also instructed me, Sam, not to use 1 Corinthians 11:23: for the Holy Communion, but Isaiah 53:4-5: so people will know about his suffering for mankind.

People do not regard his coming back and the suffering he, Jesus. Went through at the age of 33 and half years. He was in this satanic world for us. He did a lot of miracles during his time on earth. Everywhere he went he was doing good. He did no wrong, because he is a God of righteousness. Jesus is real.

St. John 1:1: in the beginning was the word, and the word was with God, and the word was God.

He came unto his own, and his own received him not. But as many as received him, to them he gave power to become the sons of God, even them that believe on his name.

St. John 1:14: and the word was made flesh, and dwelt among us, and we beheld his glory as of the only begotten of the father, full of grace and truth. At this time the music started playing and the light was shining for me to see clearly to write. The Lord loves music. On March 3, 2015, was when the angels start playing gospel music for me to wake up and write every morning at the latest 2:45 a.m.

Bye, bye, Sam. Continue the good job.

And he shall know the truth. St. John 8:30: as he spake these words, many believed on him.

Then Jesus said to those who believed, continue in the words I spoke to you, for they are life. And ye shall know the truth, and the truth shall make you free. It was the truth that led Jesus to the cross.

St. John 14:6: Jesus sayeth unto him, I am the way, the truth and the life; no man cometh unto the father, but by me.

Matthew 29:1-10: in the end of the Sabbath, as it began to dawn toward the first day of the week, came Mary Magdalene and the other Mary to see the sepulcher and behold, there was a great earthquake, for the angel of the Lord descended from heaven and came and rolled back the stone from the door and sat upon it.

My brothers and sisters, be careful of the ministers. Many of them use my name to make money. Some of them are collecting 20% instead of 10% or 15%. They will have their reward coming to them. Ministers today are more corrupt than even the people they are preaching to. Some preachers do not even give Holy Communion.

If you are not preaching the truth, then you are in trouble with Jesus after you leave this earth.

Revelation 22:12: and behold, I come quickly, and my reward is with me, to give every man according as his works shall be.

Revelation 22:19: and if any man shall take away from the words of the book of this prophecy, God shall take away his part out of the book of life, and out of the holy city, and from the things which are written in this book.

Jesus is holy and pure. That is how he wants us Christians to be for him to use us to do his work.

He went to the cross and he was victorious over death. The empty tomb was there as a witness for other to see. The two women visited the tomb and it was empty. He arose from the dead.

# THE ENDING OF THE FIRST BOOK

St. John 14:27:

Peace I leave with you. My peaces I give unto you, not as the world giveth, give me unto you. Let not your heart be troubled, neither let it be afraid.

My second coming is just around the corner. That was the promise of the father.

Acts 1:11: ...which also said, Yemen of galilee, why stand ye gazing up into heaven? This same Jesus, who is taken up from you into heaven, shall so come in like manner as ye have seen him go into heaven.

THE END

AMEN.

# BIOGRAPHY OF SAMUEL TETTEY AHULU

Samuel Tettey Ahulu is an anointed teacher of "the Lord's bible studies." He is originally from Osu, Accra, Ghana.

He attended school at anumle government school, Ghana, and then went on to study and graduate from high school in 1957.

After graduating from high school, he went on to join the Ghana navy. While he was there, he was called into the ministry by Jesus Christ to preach the gospel.

After the tour of duty, he attended Liberia Baptist theological seminary from 1975-1978.

He was the pastor of Calvary evangelical church in labadi for several years in Ghana.

Miraculously, he received a visa to visit America, where he was ordained as a minister of the gospel in Brooklyn, New York on July 17, 1982. On December 20, 1987, he was consecrated as a bishop at the new covenant holiness church in New York.

Presently, he is a pastor, evangelist, prophet; teacher and author of "the Lord's bible studies" founded September 26, 2014, and instigated by our Lord and savior, Jesus Christ.

He resides with his wife, Dorthula, in the Bronx, New York.

www.ingramcontent.com/pod-product-compliance
Lightning Source LLC
Chambersburg PA
CBHW030053100526
44591CB00008B/124